Praise for

A Computer Geek Speaks:

Unusual and interesting stories from my career as a woman in technology

"Alexandra Georgas is an artist. Her creativity flows whether she's writing poetry, song lyrics, books or computer code. As a woman recently retired from a 35+ year career in IT, I found this book to be a loving, painfully honest, and amazingly hysterical tribute to computer geeks everywhere. This is the heartfelt journey of a young woman's self-development in a largely male dominated industry. It's chock full of experience, good advice, and life lessons provided in a humorous, storied format. It's even got a lesson in fashion therapy, with hauntingly beautiful song lyrics and an Ode to the Computer Chip. I really enjoyed coming along on the ride as a naïve young woman grows into the creative, strong leader she is today. I strongly recommend A *Computer Geek Speaks* as it's full of stories that resonate, entertain, and most importantly enlighten."

- **Beverly Ryan**,
  Retired Vice President of
  Portfolio Management Office
  The Northern Trust Company

"Alexandra is a natural entertainer and storyteller. In her book, *A Computer Geek Speaks*, she has hit on one of the keys to making IT more accessible to everyone - stories! Most do not care about the technical details of databases but once you read the lyrics to her "*No Null Rap*", you will understand the power of these stories. This book should be handed to all high schoolers aspiring to enter the technology field, first because it contains valuable wisdom in a very fun package and second because all of us in IT should learn more about storytelling to help non-IT folks engage in the process more meaningfully."

- **Peter Aiken**,
  Author, Founding Director and Owner
  Data Blueprint
  Professor of Information Systems
  Virginia Commonwealth University

"*Computer Geek Speaks* is a refreshing collection of vignettes about a career in computer science, and all its idiosyncrasies - including MEN! A fun read for young women entering this field."

- **Martha Carney**,
  CEO and Founder
  Outsourced Innovation

"Very entertaining book. I would recommend *A Computer Geek Speaks* to both "techies" who have faced many of the same situations, and to non-techies who wonder what we do all day and think we don't have a sense of humor! I enjoyed reading it and certainly could relate to many of the author's experiences from floppy disc days to the fast-paced "agile" world of today. It also served as a reminder of how far we have come now that we have the ability to be connected to our phones, cars, home appliances, personal security systems, and a host of other things—all through technology."

- **Catherine Nolan**,
    President
    DAMA Chicago

"Just reading this collection of stories brought such a range of emotions including a few smiles and laughs for the joy and fun of this crazy profession we chose. The book is full of sobering reminders that there are still many challenges we need to address. Alexandra wraps each story with a little thoughtfulness, an insight to share or some good old advice. There is still much work to do in the IT profession but knowing and learning from those that have gone before us can help the next generation start their journey with their eyes wide open to the world of possibilities IT brings."

- **Wendy Rosplash**,
    Head of Information Technology and Digital
    for North America
    Kimberly-Clark

A Computer Geek Speaks

Unusual and interesting stories from my career as a woman in technology

ALEXANDRA GEORGAS

A Computer Geek Speaks:
Unusual and interesting stories from my career as a woman in technology
By Alexandra Georgas

© Copyright 2018 Alexandra Georgas

ISBN 978-0-578-44204-4

All rights reserved. No part of this publication may be reproduced, stored in a retrieval system, or transmitted in any form or by any means – electronic, mechanical, photocopied, recording, or any other – except for brief quotations in printed reviews, without the prior written permission of the author.

Published by

Alexandra Georgas

www.alexandrageorgas.com

to Allison and Dan

Table of Contents

Introduction 1
Stupid Things I Have Done... 3
Stupid Things Other People Have Done 14
Interesting People 19
Jerks... 38
Heroes.. 48
Hackers 54
Take Your Kid to Work Day....................................... 57
Sexism 60
Love Interests 65
Memorable Business Trips 74
Especially Memorable Layoffs and Relocations 83
Memorable Work Golf Outings 91
The Old Days... 94
More Interesting Stories.. 106

Introduction

I love to entertain people. Seeing folks respond to my words, songs, jokes, or stories with a smile, laugh, tears, or words of appreciation gives me a satisfaction unlike anything else. I'm not exactly sure why I love this part of life so much. I suppose it's because I didn't get enough love as a kid or something. Actually as a child, I did have a very loving mom, a super loving best friend, and two nurturing grandmothers who were quite involved in my life. No, I don't think it's that, although we can all use more love.

I've taken lots of personality analysis tests over the years and they all conclude that this is just the way I am wired. I was made to entertain, create, and be open about my life. I love to teach and help others. This is just the natural me.

My original motivation as I started jotting down these life stories was purely to entertain. Then the process of writing evolved, as it usually does, into a higher-purpose project. I hope this is a book that helps young people who are thinking about or entering the field of computer science to know some of the history and learn a little from our past. I also hope these stories show young people, and especially girls, that the technology field is not boring, but is full of relationships, adventures, love, and interesting stuff. I hope the examples provided, of both integrity and poor choices, provide insight to those coming after me in the field. I was also surprised as I wrote this to realize how much my faith was integrated into my work life. What we truly believe affects all areas of life, including our work.

I have included no names or physical characteristics of the people in these stories and almost no company names. If one of my past coworkers sees themselves in a story, if they choose to deny it's about them, I will be agreeing with them even if it is about them. Everyone gets to claim, "That's not about me." Except for me, that is.

I have left out several stories where the material was deeply embarrassing and shared to me in confidence. Even without names included, if those whom the stories are about read them, I'm sure they would be hurt and mortified. I am not about that. This is not a book to harm anyone; it is meant just to be fun, to teach, and to inspire. I hope it does that for you.

Chapter 1

Stupid Things I Have Done

Back Up Often

When I was a young, new computer programmer in 1982, I didn't have a computer on my desk. Desktops and laptops didn't exist. We only had mainframes. We had a terminal room, and we shared the terminals with our fellow programmers to enter our programs. Unlike today, when different people specialize in different functions of the job, we all did all the work—wrote the programs, tested them, and migrated them to production.

One day I had been working on a program in the terminal room, and I got stuck. I asked a more senior programmer buddy to help me. He read my code and started giving me pointers, and then the mainframe went down. I said, "What happened?" He replied, "Oh didn't you hear? They needed to take down the mainframe over the lunch hour." I asked, "Why didn't you tell me?" He countered with a scolding tone, "I thought you knew. You should have done a save." I had been working for three hours, and I hadn't saved anything. I lost all my work. I was so depressed. I went to lunch and sat in the park across the street and cried over my lost code. I never forgot the despair of losing a morning's work. I wish I could honestly say I never did this again, but I wasn't that smart.

*Me in the early years of my career.
We wore a lot of silk bow ties back then.*

Clumsy but Resourceful

One day I spilled coffee all over my computer and my floppy disk, which contained database space calculations I had worked on for hours. We used to store information on floppy disks so we could port it from one computer to another, and we used them for backups. They were 5¼–inch, soft, round disks with a thin plastic cover lined with felt. The felt was saturated with my creamy liquid. I walked over to our help desk with the dripping floppy disk in hand and asked them if they could help me. They asked, "Did you make a copy?" I had not. They just laughed and said I was out of luck.

I didn't give up. I cut open the plastic, took out the disk, patted it down with a paper towel, and then took a clean, new disk holder, cut it open, took out the unused disk, and put my coffee-smelling one in. I plugged it into the drive, and the computer was able to read it with no problems. Then I did a backup. I wrote about this story and submitted it to a computer magazine who paid me for the rights to publish. I ended up making $100 on my floppy fix!

Floppy disk

Don't Do What I Did

I used to teach people about our huge customer database, which had over 200 million customers. I admitted to everyone that I had looked up my husband's ex-wife in our database and found that she had called to get her clothes dryer serviced. Turns out the data showed that she hadn't paid her gas bill and that is why her dryer didn't work. I joked about how dumb she was in my class. Then I went to privacy training and realized I had violated company policy. Not only that, I had committed my transgression in a classroom full of coworkers! Needless to say, once I realized my stupidity I kept my trap shut about it. But I must admit that it was fun to find out a little dirt on my husband's ex. After 9/11 the government had us do queries in the database on the hijackers. That was confidential too, and here I am writing about it. I guess I'm not that good at keeping my trap shut.

Not so Funny Joke

I was presenting on our large data warehouse at a conference. I told the audience how all of my company's South American stores were owned by basically one family—and then I added, "probably bought with drug money." Oh my God, I can be so stupid sometimes! I'm sure my family-friendly company would not have liked me linking them to illegal drugs even as a joke. A coworker was in the audience and I was quite thankful she never told the bosses back at the office what a doofus I was. I realized my stupidity after I finished speaking and made sure I never repeated that error again.

Know Who You Are Meeting

I was nervous about meeting a guy I'll call Charlie, who had flown in from our Singapore office. I entered a room where there were about a dozen people, shook the hand of the only Asian looking guy in the room, and said, "You must be Charlie." He politely told me, "No, but nice to meet you." Then a giggling coworker whispered to me, "Charlie's that guy over there." Charlie was a white guy on the other side of the table. Boy did I feel stupid.

Exposure

My team went out to lunch in the dead of winter. I wore a skirt and blouse, covered by a heavy overcoat. As I took off my coat, my clothes underneath felt different, but I couldn't figure out how. Then my coworkers started cracking up while looking at my legs. I looked down, and there was my white half-slip hanging from my knees to the floor in front of everyone. My slip had slipped, and my exposed undergarment was a pretty funny sight to see. I laughed at myself, pulled my undergarment to my feet, slipped out of the slip, and put it in my purse. We giggled on our way to our table. Another one of my smooth moves.

Chinese Mess

I went to lunch at a fast-food Chinese place. When I got back to work, I headed for the ladies' room and saw that I had spilled some Mongolian beef onto my shirt. I washed out the mess, and then saw another spill a little lower on the same shirt. I washed that out and then saw another spill on my pants. Then I saw I had Chinese food on my belt, and even on my security badge. I was literally smothered in

Chinese cuisine! I had a good laugh as I continue to wash off my entire ensemble in the bathroom. Next time I go eat Chinese, I'm bringing a plastic poncho!

Pump Loss

One day I was walking around the city during my lunch hour. I was wearing these great-looking spiked-heel pumps, which I wore a lot in the early days of my career when I was young and had better balance. I stepped on a grate in the sidewalk, and one heel lodged tightly into the grate. I pulled, and—snap!—my heel broke off and fell into the abyss below. I hobbled back to the office and went barefoot at work the rest of the day, telling my coworkers about my dim-witted move. They had a good laugh. I managed to hobble to the train station that night and somehow get home. I was more bummed about losing the cute shoe than about the embarrassing walk I had to do. It was a sad day for my closet.

Torturing My Staff

When I was a new manager in my early thirties, I went to a technical conference and purchased audio tapes of the presentations I thought would help my technical staff. When I got back to the office, in my weekly team meetings I made my team of eight spend an hour each week listening to the audio tapes. In retrospect, I realize I was torturing my poor team. That was a really dumb idea. To my wonderful people who put up with me then, I am sorry. Young managers should be mentored by older ones so they don't subject their teams to extremely boring meetings as I did—unless the older managers are boring, too.

Cassette tape

Didn't Mean to Share Those Thoughts

I had to work with a guy who was very condescending and arrogant, demanded his own way, barely did anything, and was not very good at his job to boot. He eventually was laid off. I was in a meeting with him where we had to tolerate his crappy attitude, and I found him to be quite annoying. As he blabbed his offensive ideas I vented by writing in my notebook about how much I couldn't stand this guy, what a jerk he was, how he stunk at his job, and so on. Writing helped me to put a fake smile on my face and to tolerate meeting with this rude man.

Later that day a coworker came to my desk and said, "I think you left this in the room today." He handed me my notebook, which was full of my private rantings on how much I disliked that man. I was so embarrassed. My writing about him was quite raw and would likely have shocked anyone who read it. Did the man read what I wrote? Did anyone else? I had no idea. But I thought, "Well, if he saw this maybe it'll help him know how much he is offending others. He is probably clueless about that." I decided maybe it had happened for a reason and not that I was just being stupid.

No Nulls Rap

Some people in my field believed that every field in a database needed to have a value in it, and others believed that some fields could be empty—they could contain a "null" value. There were pros and cons to each position, and database professionals clung to one philosophy or another with religious fervor. In the early days of my career, I was against the null. We had a lot of inexperienced programmers who I believed probably would not remember how to work with null values in their code and would likely provide inaccurate information to our business as a result. I was so passionate about my position that I wrote a rap song about it and entertained my coworkers by performing my "No Nulls Rap" in meetings. Over the years however, we all learned how to properly handle these nulls, so I switched my religion and gave up my rap career.

No Nulls Rap

You say you need a null
To do the job right.
It'll save you lots of time
and save you lots of might.
But I've a question for you
that I think you need to hear:
why do you need a place
for nothing to be there?
You see a null is a nothing.
It's really never there.
It'll never mean something.
So why do you care?

It'll save two lines of code
But screw up the database.
You don't really need a null.

You could live with a space.
And a blank I know would do
Just as simple as can be.
So forget about the null
And we all will be happy.

No nulls, no nulls, no nulls now.
No, no nulls!
No nulls, no nulls, no nulls now.
No, no, no, no nulls!

So, give up on nulls.
I know that you can.
Or we all can give up
and go back to Fortran.
Nulls are a bad idea
especially to save code.
They're tough to understand
and hard to decode.

They don't work in equations.
Select Star ignores them too.
And selects and ad hoc queries
are really hard to do.
So keep the data clean
and insert a space
and the users will be happy
and you won't be a disgrace.

No nulls, no nulls, no nulls now.
No, no nulls!
No nulls, no nulls, no nulls now.
No, no, no, no nulls!

Despite Me

As I was graduating from college I looked very hard for a job and prayed just as hard, asking God to lead me to the best place for me. On the day of one of my seven on-site interviews, my alarm didn't go off and I overslept. I felt so stupid. I called the company human resources guy and admitted the truth: "I'm so sorry, I overslept. Would it be possible for me to still come in for the interview?" The gracious man said, as if talking to a teenager (which I wasn't that far from in age), "all right, come on in." I took the next train to the city, walked ten blocks in my open toe pumps in the slush, freezing my feet, and arrived with my hair a mess from the Chicago wind. My first interview was with people who said, "We program in Assembler," and I said to myself, "This interview is over. I'm not coding in Assembler." Assembler was an old language that I didn't enjoy coding in school. But then the HR guy told me a position had just opened in the engineering computer department. After a boring lunch with computer geeks with no social skills, I interviewed for the other position. I was thrilled. I loved programming calculus equations in the Fortran language in college. This was my dream job.

I got on the train to go home. The conductor came by and asked, "Who's going to Wheaton?" I said, "I am." He countered, "Not on this train!" Stupid young me thought that all the trains went to Wheaton! After two bus rides back to the station I got on a train to my actual town and went home.

I got a job offer from a place I had interned the previous summer, but I really didn't want to work there as it was a small manufacturing company without a lot of opportunity, and I really wanted the engineering programming job. I had prayed, and I felt this just wasn't the right job, so I turned down my only offer. The next day the engineering programming job made an offer for more money. I worked there my first thirteen years of my career and loved it.

    Moral of this story: Ask God to lead you and watch how he overcomes your own stupidity!

Chapter 2

Stupid Things Other People Have Done

The Noise

We were meeting over the phone with a consultant who was working from home, and the rest of us were in a conference room in the office. Suddenly we heard the sound of a toilet flushing. We giggled, knowing what the guy on the phone must have just done. I said, "Did you just go to the bathroom?" The guy on the phone said, "Ah, yeah, I had to go." Everyone laughed. I said, "Dude, you shouldn't do that while meeting with people." His boss found out, and he was already not doing well in his job so he was let go. I laugh every time I think about that flush sound. I guess his flush got him flushed and then he really had to go.

Trying to Be Helpful

We used to store data on 5¼-inch floppy disks and take them to and from our homes as needed. These disks were made of ferromagnetic material, so the data could be corrupted by exposure to a magnetic field. My coworker took home a disk to work on, and he told his wife, "Don't let me forget this disk in the morning." The next day, after breakfast, he asked her, "Where'd you put the disk?" His well-meaning wife answered, "Right there on the refrigerator." She had stuck it to the refrigerator using a magnet, which corrupted its contents. Poor guy lost all his work. In the office when he told us what had happened we had a good laugh. Geeks need to remember that nongeeks don't necessarily know what we know. He forgave her.

Losing His Liquid Lunch

Two coworkers went out for lunch and didn't come back until the end of the day, and both were drunk when they returned to the office. One left quickly, but the other was called into his boss's office. She confronted him for taking such a long lunch, and he started screaming so loudly at her that everyone on the floor could hear through her closed door. He yelled and yelled, and we were all very nervous about what was going to happen. After about a half hour of screaming, he left. The poor boss was so shaken.

He was a very valuable employee with special skills that were hard to replace. As a result, he was not fired but suspended for a week without pay. I think he was very fortunate he didn't end up in jail, which is where he probably should have been taken. Technical people tend to get extra forgiveness because of the high demand for our skills, whether we should or not.

Low-Budget Movie

Our department head decided to have each department meeting run by a different team each month. One team decided to make a cute video to show the rest of us what they did. The video was cheesy and gave us a little chuckle. After the video was over, they turned on the lights in the large conference room. But no one had told the audiovisual guy to turn off the video. Turns out, they had recorded their homemade movie over a teammate's porn video, and we all got to see the porn action on the very big screen. The team leader had no idea there was a porn movie displaying on the screen behind him as he tried to go on with his presentation, with waves of giggles flowing through the room. Finally, he turned around and saw what we were seeing, and turned beet red. They turned off the video. As I left the room, I joked to a coworker, "Well, I bet this will help with meeting attendance." The team leader was reprimanded and suspended for a week without pay, but not fired. We considered it the most memorable team meeting we had ever had. But it wasn't an event I necessarily wanted to remember.

Our Ex-Military Leader

I've had more job titles than I can remember. My favorite was "Database Analyst Class A." I guess I should have felt proud that I was a Class A Database Analyst, except for the fact there were no Class Bs. After I stated my title, I felt the urge to stand erect, click my heels together, and salute. Our director had served in the military, so we figured he was inspired by his combat service. We were glad he didn't make us line up and march. He did have us move to new desks on a regular basis. I guess he was protecting us from the enemy. We were safe because no one knew where anyone sat. Those were fun years.

The Company Doesn't Pay for That

A bunch of folks got sent to a fun conference in Las Vegas. They thought they could charge on their expense reports drinks they enjoyed after hours at a strip club. Really dumb move. Not only did the family-friendly company not pay for those drinks, the company made a major food policy change after that naughty deed. They told all of us we could not have any lunches or dinners catered for any meetings from that point on. The policy lasted for years. Thanks a lot, boys, for ruining lunch for all of us. At least one of them was laid off in a later reorganization. These guys just weren't too bright, so I suppose the layoff wasn't too much of a surprise. I guess what happens in Vegas doesn't stay in Vegas if it turns up on the company's tab.

Learning about Performance

I worked with a very nice guy who had a degree in English, had taken a few computer programming classes after college, and was working in our department attempting to be a technology professional. The business partner he served gave him the nickname I Mean Well. We even called him IMW for short. He had finished writing an entire system for his business customer and installed it on her computer. The thing was so slow she couldn't use it. The code had the correct logic, but he didn't know anything about how to write a system so it performs quickly. This is actually a fairly common mistake of inexperienced technology people—they write correct code, but not fast-performing code. IMW taught me a good lesson that day that made me better at my job, and I am very grateful for him and his mistake. Plus, he was a really nice guy.

Chapter 3

Interesting People

Truth Is Stranger than Fiction

I was a manager of a team of seven consultants and one employee. One of the consultants on my staff told me that three of the women on my team were members of a strange computer cult. They had spread slanderous gossip about me and others within the company, they didn't get any real work completed, and they were aloof and detached and had odd, plastic smiles plastered on their faces most of the time. Another consultant on my team knew a manager from another company who had people on his team from this cult and gave me his phone number. I called the guy, and sure enough, it was all true.

The leader was a man named Frederick Lenz. He recruited mostly young women at a university in southern California and made a deal with them: he'd finance their education if they'd switched their majors to computer science and promise to work for his company after college.

Then he'd charge a high price to companies for these young grads, who lied on their resumes to get hired. They gave him a large portion of their income, he put them in apartments, and I heard that he also had sexual relationships with many of them. They were going from one company to another—milking them for cash until management figured it out and showed them the door. Three of these members were on my staff, and they were conniving little devils. Lucky me.

In a few months I was able to hire really good people as employees, so I could get rid of the three nasties. There is a book about this cult from an ex-member, and Frederick Lenz was interviewed once on *Nightline*; I have the transcript. As they say, truth is stranger than fiction.

Teaching a Lesson

I taught an Introduction to Programming class one fall semester at the local junior college. I had a deaf girl in my class who had a sign language interpreter. There was also a super ditzy, pretty girl in the class. The ditzy girl chummed up to the nervous deaf girl. I told the class on the first day that if they turned in identical assignments both students would get zero points. On the first assignment, the ditzy girl and the deaf girl turned in identical assignments, even misspelling the same word. They both got zeroes.

Within a week, the dean of the school called me at home. Apparently, the parents of the hearing-impaired girl had called him to complain. They called me as well. I told all of them that their daughter needed to trust that she could work without the other girl and she'd be all right. She did just that and turned in B work the rest of the class. The ditzy girl struggled to get a D.

I decided that teaching at the community college was a lot of work and hassle for not a lot of pay, and I never taught a college class again. But I am thinking I might try again after I retire. Bring on those teenage minds! And their protective parents!

"Yes, And"

I used to perform songs I wrote in local restaurants and coffeehouses. I wanted to add humor to my performances, so I signed up for classes at Chicago's famous Second City school. One of the early lessons we learned in our Improvisational Acting class was called "Yes, and." In improvisation, when my partner introduces an idea, instead of negating it, I agree with it and add more to it. For example, in a scene if they say to me, "Hi Mom," then my response needs to be something like, "Hi honey. Glad you are feeling better." I agree with her decision to make me her mother in the scene and add to the scene my idea that she is getting over an illness. This promotes the movement of a scene and allows some great creative stuff to emerge.

This training has been very helpful in my IT career—when I remembered to apply it, that is. As I work on solutions with my peers, I need to see the value of their ideas, validate them, and then build onto them more thoughts I have. When I have done this, and others have been able to work with me in this way, we have developed truly solid solutions. When someone is dead set on their own idea, creative solutions are not birthed. "Yes, and" is not just for comedy. It's also an excellent way to build great computer systems.

Me performing

Close Call

A young woman on our team was in her ninth month of pregnancy with her first child. She came in around 9 a.m. and told us she was having false labor pains that morning. She said she knew they were false because there were three weeks until her due date, and, she said, "This is my first baby and first babies always come late." An older mom on our team told her, "You better go home and call your doctor." The young mom-to-be went home. She called us at 1:00 p.m. It was a boy.

Weird Church

I was always especially friendly to the cafeteria and cleaning staff. Every job is a profession if a person works hard with pride, and all people deserve attention and respect. One guy I talked with a lot as he cooked over the grill in the café invited me to attend his church with him and his wife. I agreed.

Before the service, we went to a house, where he left me with his wife and a big group of women in a living room. They zeroed in on me and told me I needed to be saved. Though I told them I already was a saved Christian, they were not satisfied and tried to convince me they had special knowledge I was not aware of. But they didn't know I had been a devoted churchgoer most of my life, so I was able to refute their unnecessary salvation requirements with my own memorized Bible verses. The ladies gave up, and then we met up with the men and went to their church.

The building was a small chapel with only about eighty people inside. The musicians played country-style songs about God. The sermon was delivered by an angry minister who seemed to be convinced that everyone needed to be confessing some sins soon. After the sermon, the people all started independently pleading to God, voicing their own prayers loudly, many with tears, shaking, and singing. It was super emotional, utter chaos. Eighty people all shouting different things at the same time in their own little worlds. I just prayed, "Lord, help me survive the rest of my time in this room." After about forty-five minutes of the completely insane vocalizations, it was over. My work friend earned his spiritual credits with his church for bringing me, but for me it was a positively disturbing experience. Lesson learned: If you go with a friend to a new church, drive separately so you can get out of there if it turns super weird.

Being a Minority

I used to supervise people who did nothing but print reports all day on our two high-speed, high-volume printers, back in the day when we printed a lot of documents. One of the guys who worked for me was a super nice man of Indian descent. Unlike the other people I had met up to that time from India, he was not of Hindu faith, but rather Christian faith. When he learned that I was a devoted churchgoer, he invited me to attend his Indian Christian church with his wife. I agreed.

The church had about three hundred people at the service, and I had to sit on the right side of the center aisle with all the women while all the men sat on the left side—very old-world. I was the only white person in the building, and when we stood to sing, I was easily a foot taller than every woman on the entire right side. As a large, tall, white woman, I felt like I was holding a neon sign saying, "Hey everyone, you have a big, tall white lady visiting your church tonight." No one in the congregation was unaware of my presence. Although I felt quite self-conscious, after the service person after person came up to me and very warmly welcomed me and thanked me for coming. I felt loved by these kind hearts. But I didn't go back to visit again. I just don't like feeling that noticed.

Good Idea

The son of a man who worked for me was getting married, and he invited me to the Hindu wedding. I was so happy to be invited and to be able to see a wedding of a different faith. During the ceremony, a voice came over the speaker in the temple, "Excuse me, but there is a car with license plate number xxxxxx with its lights on." A few minutes later another person announced over the speaker, "Excuse me, but we have refreshments in the cafeteria. Come down if you like." Meanwhile, the priest kept going with his activities, and the couple continued to follow his direction, while people left to go get food or turn off their lights. I had to chuckle. Christian weddings are shorter and more formal, and we certainly don't have announcements over the speakers during the ceremony. People don't leave in the middle to go get a sandwich. But maybe that's not a bad idea. We can eat popcorn and candy when watching a movie. Why not during a wedding? I think the Hindu folks have figured out a better way. Next wedding I go to, I'm bringing snacks.

Softball

My company had a women's softball team that competed in the local park district. I joined. I was a slow runner, was afraid to catch a fly ball, and couldn't throw a softball ten feet. I was the typical nerdy geek, with very little athletic ability. I was so bad my coach had to take me aside and teach me how to throw a ball.

But I was a good hitter. I was so good, the coach put me in the fourth position in the line-up, because I was good at hitting the other players home. Our team was quite bad, however, and the first couple of years we only won two games each season.

Then we got a new captain, and she recruited two women who did not work for our company but were incredibly great softball players. When I caught the balls they threw, they were so fast my hand burned. Their accuracy was impressive. Our company also hired a college intern who was ranked the number one women's shortstop in the nation. She was so crazy good I just wanted to sit in the stands and watch her play. That year we only lost two games. I was happy to go from being one of the best hitters on a losing team to being just an average player on a great team. It's much more fun to win as a team. This is a good analogy for the career too. Succeeding as a team is much more satisfying than succeeding in my own job while the project fails. I often have applied this valuable lesson in my career. I chose to look out for the good of the whole and not just for my own goals. When we all do this, we all win.

Me playing softball

Est

     I was in the work world only about two years when I saw one of my college professors as I was walking to work one day. I said, "Hi, remember me? I was in your COBOL and Assembler classes." He said, "Oh yes, how are you? What was your name again?" We had a pleasant, friendly chat, and I was happy that my old professor wanted to talk to me, one of his many previous students. He then invited me to have dinner with him and his girlfriend and to go to a seminar with him. I was happy he actually wanted to spend time with me, so I agreed. We exchanged numbers and set up the date and time.

     I met them in the lobby of the downtown hotel where the seminar was being held. He told me that as a new person I had to go to one room, and he and his girlfriend, who were members of the group, went to another larger room. In the smaller room the door closed, and a man started talking to the group of us, about twenty people, about the organization. He talked in vague terms about how the organization could help with anything we were struggling with, help to solve all problems, but there were no guarantees. And to get this special, powerful, unreliable help we would first have to join, which would cost a few hundred dollars. He went on incessantly for two hours. I wanted to run. There was something very wrong with this group; it was cultish. They called themselves "est."

     He finally gave us a break. As soon as the break started, the lady sitting next to me eagerly pounced on me, asking with a wide smile on her face, "What did you think?" I could see that she was a plant from the organization to work on me during the break. I said, "I am not interested," and I literally ran out the door to escape.

I went to the only place I could get away from the cult members, the bar. I sat in a booth, ordered a diet soda, and started journaling on paper my emotions and thoughts, feeling quite disturbed. An attractive man about my age and wearing a very nice suit walked up to me and asked, "May I sit with you?" I said, "Sure, if you like." He sat, and calmly and kindly said to me, "I see you are writing there. What are you writing about?" I told him what I had just been through and how it was very bothersome to me. The kind man listened with loving eyes and encouraged me: "Well, it sounds like you made the right decision to get out of there." That was just what I needed to hear. His affirmation soothed my anxiety. And then he dismissed himself and was gone in what felt like an instant. Looking back, I have always wondered if I had entertained an angel unaware, as the Bible says, meaning that there are angels who look like people to us, who come and help us when we really need it. For me, he was an angel.

After the others finished their session we all went to dinner at an Italian restaurant. My former professor's girlfriend seemed to be very angry at me for walking out and not signing up to her cult. I remembered my angel's affirmation, kept quiet, and waited for the evening to end. I never saw that professor again. Later I read that the group was considered a cult. I'm glad my well-dressed, handsome angel helped me that day to not let these people manipulate me into losing money to their lofty and vague promises. I'm very thankful to this day.

Helping a Hothead

One of the guys we worked with had quite the temper. He tried to keep himself calm, but from time to time he would start getting excited, his voice would get louder, higher pitched, and we'd all try to de-escalate him. We did a pretty good job. We did well, that is, until the guys took him out golfing. He became so frustrated he threw his entire set of golf clubs into the pond and stomped away. After he left, the guys went into the pond and got his clubs out for him, and they later gave them back to him when Mr. Angry had calmed down. Now that's teamwork.

The Cheese Tray Man

I worked with a guy who hated shopping so much that on Christmas day he would not have any presents for his family. Instead, he'd go out the day after Christmas and buy each family member a discounted cheese and sausage tray. If I did that to my family, I wouldn't get any presents. They would boycott me for sure. He must have had a forgiving family. Or one that really loved cheese.

More Common than You'd Think

I wrote a book about my journey of recovering from growing up with a mother who had developed schizophrenia, *Mom & Me: My Journey with Mom's Schizophrenia*. It was scary for me to let everyone know about my personal story, especially at work. I feared people would gossip about me, saying mean things like, "I bet she has it too," or "No wonder she loses her cool sometimes." I took the chance anyway, and I found that I had still been feeling shame about her, and that the shame was relieved by my openness.

My openness caused others in the office to tell me about their own mental illness or that of their family members. A woman told me how her father, on a bipolar high, spent money and time on ridiculous, wasteful projects. Another woman told me of her mother with schizophrenia who wandered off from her nursing home and got lost from time to time. Two women had the same story of sadness over their brothers with schizophrenia who were both living on the streets, homeless. One guy's sister had bipolar disorder. Another man's brother had committed suicide. A coworker suffered from obsessive-compulsive disorder (OCD), another from bipolar disorder. Another's mom had severe OCD, another had a daughter with bipolar, and another man worried much about his teenage daughter with depression. Yet another coworker had lost her precious teenage son to suicide after he had fought depression for years.

Mental illness affects the families of people in the computer technology field at the same rate it affects those of people in any other profession or demographic. I'm so glad I took the risk and opened up about my story, because I was able to lend an empathetic ear to these coworkers and hopefully relieve some of their lingering difficult emotions. Speaking your truth heals.

A Gift

In my first job out of college I sat next to a woman who had arguments with her boyfriend on her phone during business hours. I didn't listen to the specifics, but the fact that she was arguing couldn't be denied. One of the guys on our team loved to watch the soap opera *All My Children* so much that he taped every episode and watched them daily. But he loved even more listening to our coworker's daily drama. We had our own private, melodramatic show.

After she broke up with the boyfriend, he showed up at the back of her house one day and shot at her through her bathroom window, leaving bullet holes in the house. Fortunately, she was not injured. He went to jail. She was quite shaken by the event but recovered.

She also had issues with overspending and was terribly in debt. I felt sorry for her. Her life sounded chaotic, stressful, and not like much fun.

I prayed a lot for her. One day I felt a strong urge to help her out financially. I believe this was God nudging me. The next day I went into work and handed her an envelope with three one-hundred-dollar bills in them and said to her, "I think God wanted me to give you this. It's to let you know He loves you and to get you started on getting out of trouble."

She looked stunned and whispered a sheepish, "Thank you." I left her cube and sat back at my desk.

She opened the envelop and loudly exclaimed, "Sandy! I can't accept this. What are you doing?" I went back into her office. She had tears in her eyes. "I just can't accept this."

I pushed, "No, I think you should. I really want you to have it. I do believe God led me to do this, so you need to take it. Just remember He loves you, and there is mercy and grace for you." She cried and gave me a warm hug, with a hearty, "Thank you!"

She did end up getting out of debt, finding and marrying a much nicer man, and doing a lot better in her life. She told me years later, "I will never forget what you did." I'm glad I followed the nudging. It feels good to show someone else shocking love. And then it was even more gratifying to see her do better in her life. It was very rewarding to be used by God to help another soul find peace.

Chapter 4

Jerks

Not Just a Figure of Speech

I was working with a project manager who was very mean. He was condescending and angry and put us all down all the time. Sadly there have been a few of these in my career. At that time, I also was experiencing a painful case of sciatica that just wouldn't go away. Then on a Tuesday he was suddenly gone. The gossip was that he got canned. That was the last day I had the sciatica. He had literally been a pain in my butt.

Not Quite Hired

I was going to our local junior college and had fallen in love with programming and knew that was what I wanted to do. I wanted to start getting real work experience in my field. I applied for a part-time programming job on the school job board. The owner of the company said he would hire me starting right after Christmas. I quit my job as a crew member at McDonald's, which I had done for over three years by then. A month went by, then two, and the guy kept saying he wasn't ready for me to start. The jerk didn't have a job for me. So I went back to work as a crew member at McDonald's. My boss there was mad that the guy had done that to me. I made sure my future job offers were in writing before I quit my existing job. My junior college experience taught me more than how to code programs.

Fighting for My Position

I had a meeting with a director of another IT area. I felt the need to pray for God to help me do a good job in the meeting. Afterward, the director asked me if I would be interested in a position on his team, learning to be a data architect. I told him I'd think about it. I told my boss about the position, and at first he said, "That sounds like a great opportunity. You should go for it."

I met with the director, who told me more about the job, and it sounded very interesting, so I told my boss I'd like to transfer. My boss then told me I was not going to be allowed to because *his* boss had told him I couldn't go. We were on a hiring freeze, and if I left they would not be able to fill the vacancy. I was really mad. I asked him if I could speak with his boss. He said, "Go right ahead, but I don't think you'll be able to convince him."

I went to see his boss and said to him, "If you were the VP of IT, and you knew that there was a hiring freeze, which meant that your staff was becoming more limited, would you rather put your scarce talent on what you call the most important area (which was the new area), or in my old job?" The reluctant boss knew I had a winning argument and that I'd go over his head if necessary. The transfer was allowed. I learned how to be a data architect, and I have done that job for most of my career and have loved it. Since that time, whenever I have had a staff member ask to transfer I have always encouraged them and helped them. I know what it's like to have to fight for a new job, and I don't want to put good people through that.

Bad VP

A position opened to be a director of master data management at my company. Having spent many years working in that field, I thought I was qualified and would enjoy the position. I applied for the job. I interviewed for the inner company change and heard nothing. My boss told me the vice president of my area didn't want me to transfer. She didn't want to lose me.

I cornered the vice president one day on the way to a department meeting. I told her how much it would mean to me to be considered for the position and asked if she could recommend me for the job. She seemed to be flustered that I was so bold as to ask for her help—and to ask on the way to a meeting instead of setting up an appointment with her.

The VP not only didn't help me get the position, she complained to my boss that she didn't like it that I had talked to her about it in the hallway. She even had him write in my annual review months later that for the entire year I lacked communication skills, all because of that five-minute conversation with her. I was so mad. Not only did she stop me from advancing in my career, she forced a very unfair and inaccurate assessment of my work for the year. At that time the company used to send the employees an anonymous survey to see if we were happy in our jobs. I wrote that openness was discouraged in our department and that I would never ever speak to my VP again. And I didn't. I also lasted years longer at that company than she did.

I find it especially sad when women don't help other women in the workplace. Out of one side of our mouths we complain about a glass ceiling and being underpaid, and then out of the other side of our mouths we compete with our sisters, backstab them, and get in their way. Perhaps women are hurting women more than men are. Ladies, let's choose to help our work sisters, not harm them. Let's be the ones who promote one another and make the work world a better place for our daughters.

Not So Funny

On my second day of work at a new company, the guy who sat next to me told me that Fridays were Hawaiian shirt day. So, on my first Friday I wore a bright, colorful, flower-filled Hawaiian shirt. I looked around and realized I was the only person in the entire department wearing one. I asked the guilty coworker about it. He laughed and claimed that he was wearing a Hawaiian shirt, but his shirt was solid gray. As time went on, I learned that this guy had tried to get my position, but I got it instead, and he was hired for a lower-level position. He turned out to be a really hard person to work with until they finally laid him off. I guess the Hawaiian shirt prank was my warning of the years of torment that were to come. But I did look good in my shirt that day.

Recruiter Thugs

    I was looking for a new job and had an appointment with two guys from a recruiting company. We met at a hotel lounge. The guys had me sit in a chair in a corner and the two of them sat in large chairs opposite me, blocking my ability to exit. They drilled me on my skills, goals, desires, and so on in an aggressive interrogation style. I started feeling verbally attacked, like these guys were ganging up on me. They were not nice. After a few minutes of their aggression, I got up and practically crawled over them, then hurried out the door. Some people are just stupid. I had highly sought skills at the time, and these guys thought a good way to work with me was to be condescending and high-pressure. I'm glad I listened to my gut and got out of there. I suppose that's one reason we used to call these people head hunters.

Hang-Up

I was working with two men who both did the same job I did—they were fellow data architects—and both seemed convinced that they were superior to me. I'll call them Cheech and Chong. Cheech had an especially condescending attitude; he was later let go in a layoff.

Late on a Friday afternoon Cheech scheduled a meeting at eight o'clock on a Monday morning, which was normally not done and was not very considerate of others. I let him know that I would be dialing in from home because I was scheduled to work from home that day. He sternly replied, "It will be impossible for you to participate then." People worked from home all the time and successfully participated in meetings over the phone, so this was an odd declaration. I replied, "Well I'm not going to not participate."

On Monday morning I phoned into the meeting. I heard the conversation well and noticed they had made an incorrect statement. I spoke up and clarified for them. They just kept talking like I hadn't said anything. I thought, "Oh goodness, they are either ignoring me, or the volume is so low they can't hear me." I spoke up, "Hello? Can you guys hear me?" Nothing. I said it again, "Hello? Can you hear me at all?" Next thing I heard was the sound of their phone receiver hitting the unit and then a dial tone. They had hung up on me. I was shocked. I couldn't believe these jerks would do that to me.

I called back, and no one picked up. I then called the project manager and let him know what had happened and that I was not allowed to be part of the meeting. He helped me, and I was finally able to call back in. Chong said, "I hung up on you." With no apology or explanation. He had done it on purpose! I was even more flabbergasted.

The games grown men play. When they laid off Cheech, I wasn't surprised. He just didn't play well with others. Arrogant game-players typically do not last long in good companies. Fortunately, I didn't have to work with Cheech much, and Chong by himself was not that hard to deal with. He just acted badly around Cheech.

Eventually I was free from both when I changed jobs and went to a new company. I worked with more arrogant, condescending people in my career, but these are the only two bozos who hung up on me during a business call.

Betrayal

I was a manager of eight database administrators, which we referred to as DBAs. My boss brought on two additional high-priced consultant DBAs to work directly for her on special projects. These guys did seem to know their stuff, so I didn't mind, except they didn't really let me know what they were doing. Turns out, one was campaigning for my position. His wife was pregnant and was pressuring him to stop his consultant travel and she wanted him to keep earning a high enough salary so they could keep their fancy house. He was telling my boss how much more qualified he was than me, and how he should have my job. Eventually my boss agreed, demoted me, and made me work for this man about ten years my junior. It was a very hard blow. He then treated me very badly, putting me down, trying to find fault in everything I did.

I complained openly about my unjust situation. One of the older guys on my team took me aside and told me this story. "There was a little bird. Someone shot at the little bird with a BB and it got knocked of the tree and fell to the ground injured. It flapped around wildly, trying to get back up. Then a dog came along and pooped on the bird. The bird flapped around with even more fervor. A cat then came along and ate the bird. If the bird would have just stayed quiet, waited until it healed, it could have flown away unharmed." I knew I was the bird in the story, and I was making things worse by being vocal. I took his advice and got real quiet.

I looked for a new job and finally found an ideal position at another company and left. As I walked out of the building I literally took off my shoes and shook the dust off of them.

Another woman on my staff there was and still is a good friend of mine. She told me the guy who had campaigned for my job was the worst boss she ever had, that he was probably on cocaine considering the way he acted, that he didn't stay long, and that his wife divorced him. Our boss, who had made this mess happen, was moved, so she no longer had direct reports. My friend also told me she thought I was a good boss. That was nice to hear.

The young mean boss didn't just betray me. He betrayed himself by choosing a path of dishonesty. Even with all of this, I still wish for him to learn, grow, find love again, and become a better person. I know he was a young man making mistakes. I made mistakes in my life as well. I have forgiven him and myself. I truly hope he becomes a wiser, happier older man as I have hopefully become a wiser older woman. Time does heal the hurt even from jerks.

Good View, Bad Boss

I once had a corner office on the top floor of an office building, and my view was of the Chicago river and the beautiful Chicago architecture—best office of my career. However, it was one of my most miserable times. My boss was a young, insecure jerk who used his knowledge as a weapon, constantly trying to put me down and make himself feel qualified. I didn't last long. I found another job and moved on.

People usually don't leave jobs or offices. People leave bad bosses. And in the world of technology, most managers lack the people skills needed to be good bosses. So we all change jobs a lot, hoping to find a really nice, smart, good boss. But guess what? That boss doesn't have any openings because the people are so happy they won't leave. And that's the sad world of IT. If you have a good boss, by all means stay at that job and be super nice to that boss. You are in the world of green grass. Enjoy.

View from my best office but one of my worst jobs

I've Been the Jerk

On more than one occasion during my career, I know I've been the jerk. I have overreacted to people, been stubborn about my ideas, had a rude tone, acted arrogant, spoken with foul language, lost my patience, gossiped, and hurt others. My worst behavior came during times when I was feeling very stressed because of a heavy workload, a bad boss, challenges in my personal life, or a threat to my position. But if I were a better leader, I wouldn't take my unfortunate situations out on others. To all who have put up with me when I've been the jerk, I am so sorry.

A good friend told me once, "Not everything is magenta. Some things are mauve." I've been in a lifelong battle with myself to remember that it's just work, and I don't need make a big deal out of everything. I hope as I move into my senior years, I can have better success reining in my passion. Or perhaps I should just keep it for my causes, like helping others less fortunate than myself, and leave my poor coworkers alone. That sounds like a good recovering-jerk plan.

Chapter 5

Heroes

Vietnam Vet Trainer Man

I once worked with a Vietnam veteran who trained me to be a data architect. He was very upbeat, funny, always positive, forgiving to difficult people, and just a great person to work with. He said two phrases nearly daily to us in Vietnamese. The first I learned to say, which sounded like "Toy See Ghit Ban," meant "I will kill you" in Vietnamese. His other saying was, "Tomorrow we go on operation such and such and kill many VC" That was a long sentence so I never learned that one.

One night he was having a bad nightmare about being in combat. He dreamed the enemy had caught him in a net, and he was not able to get out. His wife woke him, and he found that he had somehow gotten into her drawer of pantyhose, which felt like the net in his dream. He and his wife cracked up when they realized he was being attacked by her pantyhose in the night. When he told me about this dream, I was glad to get a glimpse of what a vet had to experience, and happy he could laugh at the humor of it. He was my hero.

Me and a Vietnam vet coworker

Sneaky Vietnam Vet Man

Our team had a social outing at a local laser tag place. We divided into two teams, and in the dark, with loud, pounding music, we ran around shooting our lasers at each other and tried to get to the opposing team's home base to score the big points.

After the game was over, the man with the highest points was a project manager on our team who had served in Vietnam. During the game, we had never seen him, but his score was impressively higher than those of the rest of us. It was a hint of what he had experienced in his past and showed how he had survived and was able to return after the war. I had a new respect for him after that day, and a little fear. I made sure to not make him mad.

Transformative Lunch Hour

I made friends with a woman at work whose family was quite wealthy, and she liked to wear fairly high-fashion outfits to the office. I remember one black dress she wore that had a dramatic cape. It was fun to just see what she was going to wear every day.

Another friend from work and I were planning a vacation together to Florida. I told her I didn't know what I would wear, because I was overweight, and I didn't have anything appropriate for the warm weather of the South. She had the fashion friend take me out shopping on a lunch hour. The fashionista parked me in the dressing room and brought item after item for me to try on. Before this day I wore a lot of beige, cream, and white. I was hidden in my neutral attire. My fashion-frenzy friend had me try on orange, turquoise, and other bright colors. I was so happy to see that I looked good in the items she picked. I spent $800 in that one hour of shopping with my wealthy friend and obtained a full wardrobe for Florida. I went back to work a changed woman. I never wore the bland colors again. A lunch hour of fashion therapy truly changed my life.

Years later I got to do this same therapy for my stepdaughter. It was her birthday and Valentine's Day, and she and her boyfriend had gotten into a fight. I took her out shopping. I had her pick nearly everything in a store and told her to try it on. Then I bought for her everything that she liked. I was so happy to see how happy she was. I knew how great it was for someone to encourage you to let yourself have nice clothes and look good. I learned from my fashionable friend at work that fashion therapy truly is transforming and therapeutic.

In the Minutes

We worked with an older man who would announce every day when there was less than an hour before quitting time, "Well, we're in the minutes." We loved hearing him say that. It was our daily reminder that the day was winding down and soon we would get to go home. We liked him.

Praying IT Men

I had lost my husband to cancer, two years had passed, and I felt ready to start dating. I knew that finding someone to spend the rest of my life with was no easy task, so I prayed a lot for God to lead me.

A guy at work organized a weekly prayer group, which I joined. I was the only women in the group of all computer technology men. Every week I asked them to pray for God to lead me to a good man to love. And they did.

After months of prayers and me dabbling in the dating world, I met my new husband. I do believe our prayers opened this blessing. I believe these kind-hearted IT brothers of mine helped me to be directed to the man I am so happy to spend the rest of my life with. Some geeks are really beautiful people. These men were, and I'm so thankful for them.

A Wonderful Inspiration

I met a very nice, older woman at work. She told me that she had been raped and brutally beaten years before. When she was a young woman, she was hitchhiking across the country, and she was abducted. The police told her that most women beaten as badly as she was do not survive. She was hospitalized for months, but she recovered. She shared that in retrospect she is thankful that although it was a terrible crime, it helped her grow closer to God, and that had been a huge help in her life. Her openness was a great gift to me; I learned how faith can help a person overcome something so horrendous. She was my hero.

Hurricane Gilbert

We had a women's Bible study group that met on our lunch hours at the office, as well as a men's Bible study group. One of the ladies who started the women's group quit her job at our company to be a missionary in Kingston, Jamaica, with her husband and four children. Hurricane Gilbert hit the island; it starting at one end and traveled directly over the island to the other side. The poor country was devastated. Our friend wrote to tell us what they needed. One of the guys leading the men's Bible study organized a relief project, and the rest of us in the two Bible study groups donated everything on our friend's list. I went to a camping store and bought water filtration tablets, batteries, canned food and dried edibles. Our organizing man found out the maximum amount of luggage he could bring: two checked bags and two carry-ons. He packed minimal clothes and filled the rest of his luggage with food and supplies. He got on a plane and headed for Kingston.

When he arrived at the airport in Jamaica, he witnessed utter chaos, with long lines of people trying to get off the island. He pushed through with his four suitcases of relief. He was proud to see large crates of relief aid stamped with big black letters, "United States of America." Our country came through immediately, which never made the news.

Our missionary friend used some of the supplies for her family of six, but also gave away many of them. There was so much need around her, she had to help.

Those of us in the Bible Study groups were comforted to know we had helped people not just by writing a check to a relief organization, but by delivering supplies via our coworker to a country in great need. The joy for us lasted for a very long time. It feels great to team up to make a miracle for someone. And we did.

My missionary friend and supplies we sent

Chapter 6

Hackers

Not A Winner

Our company had a sweepstakes that people could enter online via a website that we provided. My team reported to our business partners how many entries we had received each day. We saw a spike in entries one day during the sweepstakes. We dug into the data and saw that one email address had 13,000 entries that day. We hypothesized that someone had built a computer program to automate entries into our site. However, the hacker wasn't that clever since he had used his full name in the email address he employed for his hack. I did a Google search on his name and email address and found him on Facebook, posing in a photo with his home computer system, of which he was obviously very proud. His not-so-hidden profile revealed the name of the town where he lived and indicated that he was a grad student in computer science.

What he didn't know was that our system had a maximum number of entries allowed per day per email address, so he was automatically disqualified and didn't win the grand prize—a car. We didn't need to do anything since we had built in limits to protect from hackers. When teaching others, I have used his example as a reminder that customer-facing systems will have people trying to hack in, and security measures must always be present. I am happy that the customer-facing systems I worked on have never been successfully hacked. Sometimes we IT geeks get it right.

Password Practices

Our system monitoring programs alerted us of an unusually high amount of rapid activity on our system. We investigated the transaction logs and saw that someone was trying to hack into our website. We could see that this person had a program that was generating email addresses and trying to log into our site with these addresses, probably employing a set of commonly used passwords. Our site was just for people to sign up to receive emails, so we had no information of much value to the intruder. We figured the hacker was probably recording which email and password combinations worked on our site so they could then try the combinations on other sites—like online retail websites to make purchases, or banking sites to steal money. A lot of people use the same passwords on many sites, making them vulnerable.

We traced our system and found the IP addresses the hacker was using and set a block so the intruder was no longer able to access our website, installed better anti-hacker software, and then continued to monitor to be sure the hacker was disabled. I felt proud that our team was able to protect our customers. Moral of the story: Do not use the same passwords for banking and shopping as you do to sign up for marketing emails.

Chapter 7

Take Your Kid to Work Day

Bus Driver: One; Me: Zero

I was standing at a corner in the city waiting for the light to change to green. The streets were wet from a recent snow that was in the process of melting. There was a huge puddle of slushy gray water filling in a large pothole at the curb right in front of me. A bus came along and, as if the driver was hoping to score points, hit that puddle in full force and sent up a splash that drenched my entire body, including my head. I was dripping with cold, wet, dirty slush. It had been Take Your Child to Work Day, and a man I worked with was standing near me with his cute little daughter. The two laughed so hard I thought they were going to pull a muscle. I just looked at them, smiled, and said, "Funny, huh? Watch out for buses little girl." I guess she did learn something from her trip to the office with Daddy: Don't be stupid like the lady at the corner who got all wet. Watch out for the buses!

Being an Inspiration

For Take Your Child to Work Day I brought my youngest step-son to work with me. I was a data architect at that time: I figured out how to store data fields in a big database, using a methodology called normalization to organize information and data relationships on the basis of set theorems. This was the job I did most of my career.

I brought my step-son to one of my meetings and let him draw on the whiteboard with colored markers while we did our business. Then I let him play games on my computer for a while. I had him do some simple Excel copy and pastes for me. We had lunch at our amazing, huge cafeteria. He basically got to goof off all day while I worked. On the way home he told me, "When I grow up, I want to be a data architect." I cracked up. He had no idea of what I did, but in his mind, it was drawing colorful pictures on the whiteboard, copying stuff in Excel, and playing games. Actually, that is a lot of what I did at work. I guess he did learn something.

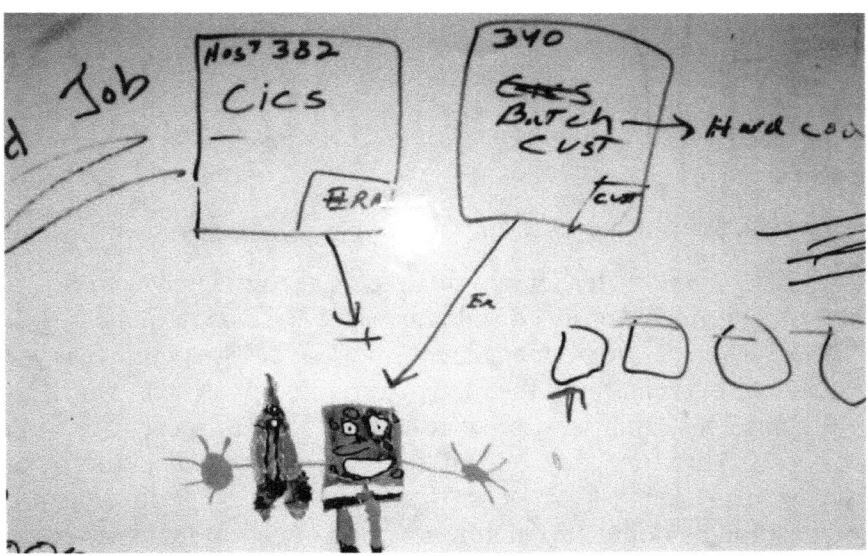

A drawing my kid did at work. We used the characters to represent components of the computer system.

Chapter 8

Sexism

Nasty Accusation

I was the leader of a small team of four. I had to work with a group of nasty consultants who were raking in a high hourly rate, telling our executives how stupid we employees were, and claiming that they were doing all the work themselves, although we were the ones doing most of the work. Then one day one of the consultants called me a "Monica Lewinsky." He was accusing me of getting my position by doing sexual things, which of course I had never done in my life. I was shocked that he had taken a risk with his career by making such a statement in violation of human relations policy. I told my boss, who did nothing about it. We both knew his contract would be up within a few months and he'd be gone. But still, he shouldn't have been able to work there another day. The technology field can be too tolerant of very bad behavior because of the high demand for and low supply of computer professionals. And so I paid the price that day.

Male Ignorance

We had a boss who liked to talk so much we gave him the nickname "Core Dump." A core dump was when the mainframe printed hundreds of pages of the system's inner contents, in difficult-to-interpret numbers. This occurred after programming code with severe errors was executed. Sometimes we intentionally caused a core dump to debug our programs, and once upon a time I knew how to read them.

A coworker told me that after she let Core Dump know that she was getting married, he asked her if she was going to quit after the wedding. I guess in his thinking married women didn't work. We were surprised not only that he had such an antiquated idea, but that he thought it was OK to voice it. It turned out she worked for decades and is still working today. He isn't.

They Are Hard on the Women Leaders

One company had a reorganization and let go of a lot of the middle management. They laid off a woman who was the best senior director we had ever had—far better than any other leaders of our department. She helped people to get along, had over twenty years of experience with the company, and used that experience to help us make good decisions. She was fun, kind-hearted, and giving, but she had backbone when she needed it and was quite wise. Our team was both shocked and disturbed when she was let go. We knew the company had gotten that decision so wrong. I have seen many far less qualified men in those same positions not only stick around but get promoted, but a stellar woman like her was dumped. There is a glass ceiling for women in technology, and that day we all experienced it as more like a career sledgehammer, striking down a very talented woman. This was one reason I was reluctant to pursue the management track. IT management is not an easy career, especially for woman leaders.

You Say She Did What?

We were getting a new senior director, who was a very attractive woman with long blond hair. A male coworker of mine told me she wasn't going to be any good and said he had heard how she got her position, then then acted out choking on a penis. I scolded him and told him he should not say such a rotten thing, and that I was sure it wasn't true. I had already worked a little with the woman, and I thought she was intelligent and qualified. She turned out to be an OK leader, with some strengths and some weaknesses. I never told her or HR what my coworker had said. The guy who said it was one of my gossip providers, and usually his information was kinder and more reliable than on that day. Although he had displayed a lack of good judgment, he was someone I liked a lot. I didn't want to get him in trouble, so I didn't report the incident. A woman in computer technology has to pick her battles to survive. My choice that day was to let that one go, but perhaps that makes me part of the sexism problem. How many other people did he spread that bad rumor to? In hindsight, I'm not sure my inaction was the right response. I hope other women don't follow my example in that regard.

A Disturbing Day at the Beach

A guy at work invited me and others to a day at the beach. I didn't know him very well, but as a young, single, extroverted woman, I thought a beach party sounded great. I had my weight down at this time, so I wore a sexy swimsuit and looked awesome.

A skinny, average-looking coworker of mine whom I didn't know well warmed up to me at the beach party. We chatted, and then he told me his boat was nearby and asked me if I'd like to see it. I said, "Sure." He led me through some woods to an area that was not close to the beach, but was a private, hidden cove. I had a sinking feeling in my stomach. This didn't look safe to me.

His restored vintage boat was a quite nice. He pointed out the beautiful wood panels and told me of the work he had put into it. He was creepy, and I wanted to run. Finally, I told him, "I'm really uncomfortable right now and I'd like to go." He replied, "Yeah, you are? OK, you can go."

I walked back to the beach area feeling shaken by the near miss with this icky guy. He went straight to the men's room. After he emerged, he didn't talk to me for the rest of the day. I felt shaken. I feared that I had nearly been raped.

After I returned home, I talked to my brother about this near assault, trying to shake off the feelings that still loomed days after the event. My brother kindly soothed me, "You took care of yourself, and you didn't let that happen." His words calmed me. I did take care of myself. I wished someone would take care of that creepy man.

My Mantra

"Don't let others define you." I read these words once upon a time and realized that the mantra would help me a lot as a woman in a male-dominated career field. Some men I worked with seemed to lack experience with technical women like myself. They seemed to have the false belief that women couldn't be good at technology. They made statements implying that they assumed I was less knowledgeable and experienced than I was. Rather than battling these men, I just ignored them and repeated my mantra to myself, "Don't let others define you." I knew who I was and what I knew, and I didn't need them to know it for it to be true. I just stayed true to myself, let them think what they chose to think, and let my work speak for my brain. And it did.

Chapter 9

Love Interests

Handsome Influence

A certain engineer used to come by my cubicle every day to socialize. We were both young and single. He was so handsome, and he had a great sense of humor. I had a total crush on him. But we only had lunch once, when he took me out in his fancy Corvette. He liked me, but I was a scared church girl, and he wasn't a scared church guy. He was very into good money management, and he told me to put 6 percent of my pay into the company 401K to get the 100 percent company match. He was so cute I did it right away, and have done it ever since. The strategy has helped me tremendously to be prepared for retirement. All thanks to a cute engineer I never dated.

Practicing My Flirting

I had watched a video called "How to Flirt." I was such a geek I really didn't know how. I decided to try out the new material. As I talked to a friend of mine at work, a handsome, muscular, very nice, unattached black engineer, I swirled my hair and smiled. I could hardly believe it when he asked me out. "Wow, this flirting stuff works," I thought. He and I just went out for a short while—maybe about five dates. Then his ex-girlfriend found out he was going out with me, and she told him she wanted him back. He ended it with me, and right after he resumed dating her she dumped him. But I just used my new flirting tactics on the next nice guy I was interested in and moved on. I decided not to end my new flirting career.

Attempted Pickup 1

I was having lunch at a soup and salad fast-food place near my office in the city. A well-dressed, attractive, professional man asked if he could sit with me, and I welcomed him to do so. We chatted warmly for a while, and then he asked if he could take me to dinner sometime. I was quite surprised that a stranger I had just met in a casual lunch place would actually ask me out. I also felt really nervous about having dinner with a man I had met in this way. I wasn't a big dating risk taker so this was a bit beyond my comfort level. Although he seemed very nice and normal and probably was a great catch, I just didn't feel like I could have dinner with him. In retrospect, I wish I had. He might have been a really good man. But computer geek girls don't always have a lot of game. At least this one didn't.

Attempted Pickup 2

I was briskly walking to the train after a day of work, wearing a white lacy dress. I was in my twenties at the time. A man started walking next to me at the same fast pace and declared to me, "You remind me of my girlfriend back in Tanzania." Now that is an interesting pickup line. I tried to brush him off, saying flatly, "That's nice." But the fast-walking man would not relent. He kept talking to me as we walked, and he asked me out. If I hadn't had heels on, I think I would have started running to get away from him. But I just kept saying "No thank you" and continued walking. He finally gave up, and I was free. I tried to decide if this was something to be upset about or proud of. I mean, hey, I must have looked pretty good that day if a man just walked up to me on the street and tried to get me to go out with him. I decided that was the case, and not that I was almost abducted by some dangerous dude.

A Date with a Pest

I was taking night classes toward my master's degree in computer science. A guy in my class liked to ask a lot of annoying questions in class and had the foulest mouth I had ever heard. He followed me and my friend to the coffee area on our break and chummed up to us both. Week after week he kept asking me to go out after class for a drink, and I refused week after week. But the man was relentless. After weeks of his determination, I agreed to get a cup of coffee with him after class.

We walked to a coffee shop together, and the man talked incessantly, with nearly every other word a swear word. My stomach turned. I was polite and kind to him but knew this was a guy I didn't even want to even be friends with, let alone date. After an hour of mostly me listening to him swear, he asked me if he could see me again. I told him I didn't think we were a match. The clueless talker asked, "Why?" Guys who ask why you don't want to date them are usually guys who want to debate with you that you should want to date them, not realizing that makes you dislike them even more. He was one of those. I kept it vague and just kept saying, "We are not a match." He finally gave up and agreed to end the time together.

He needed me to drop him off at the el train he took to get home. As I drove him there, bright red and blue lights flashed in my rearview mirror. He said, "Oh, you're not allowed to drive on State Street. Only service vehicles are allowed." I told him, "It would have been nice of you to not direct me this way then!" On top of having to listen to his profanity lava flow, I got a ticket as well. I learned a lesson though: don't go out with a guy just because he pesters you. Instead, just tell him the truth directly so he can have a chance to learn how he is getting it wrong.

Small World

Before there was internet dating, there were personal ads in the newspapers. I answered one and agreed to meet the guy. He wrote that he was very handsome and a Christian. I wasn't especially looking for a handsome man, but when I met him, I could see he didn't have a very accurate view of himself. He was quite homely.

During the meal he was mean to the waitress. He was very picky about his order and then snapped, "You won't get it right anyway!" He told me that his mother had had four husbands, and about his crappy childhood. I already knew when I witnessed his rudeness to the waitress that I was not going to be dating him. He was critical and not nice. But I decided to just listen with empathy and be kind to him.

As we parted he said he'd like to see me again, and I was vague.

The next day I went to work and told a good friend and coworker about my date. We were so surprised when we realized my blind date, whom I had met via a newspaper ad, had been her roommate. She told me, "He thinks he's real attractive, and he's arrogant and mean." I said, "Yes, that's the guy." She told me he was hard to live with and she had to kick him out. It's a small world.

After a couple of days, he called me and asked me out again. I told him politely, "I don't think we are a match." He persisted and kept asking what made me think that. He wouldn't just give up and leave me alone. So I told him that my work friend had told me he was not nice to her, and I saw that he wasn't kind to the waitress either. He got very angry and said, "Your friend is a messed-up woman and you are the most overweight woman I have ever gone out with." I wasn't even very heavy at that time. He just confirmed his jerkiness. He was a wounded and angry man, and I suspect he never found love. But I did.

Southern Gentleman

I was about twenty-three or so, and I got to go on a business trip to our Houston office with three coworkers, two of whom were also younger, single women. After work one day we all went out to the bars to have a little fun. A very handsome young guy asked me to dance, and I happily agreed. I ended up hanging out with this fine, polite southern young man the whole evening. We talked, danced, and had a wonderful time together. He was a perfect gentleman.

He worked for three months at a time on the off-shore drilling rigs and was home for his rest time. He told me he made great money, but it meant having to be away from everyone for long periods of time. I felt very drawn to this kind-hearted man. After the bars closed, he drove me in his fancy blue BMW to my hotel and gave me a sweet kiss good night. We exchanged phone numbers, and I promised to stay in contact with him. I was stricken with attraction.

I could barely sleep all night, thinking of this man who drew me in like a love magnet. The next morning on the plane ride home, I had a dazed look in my eyes as I thought about him.

I never called him. I decided it was not realistic to date a man in Texas while I lived in Chicago. It was hard to say no to my feelings, but I made myself be practical. And this is one of my life regrets—not giving love a chance. If I did it again, I would have called him and given us a chance. Go for love. Be impractical. You never know.

Not Quite What I Prayed For

I had a crush on one of my coworkers. One Friday I prayed in the morning at work, "Lord, if he is a good man for me, please have him ask me out." Five minutes before quitting time he walked up to my cubicle and said, "What are you doing this weekend?" Clueless me said, "Oh tonight I'm doing this and this, tomorrow this and that, Sunday church, blah blah blah. What are you doing?" He answered, "Tonight I'm playing basketball with my friends, tomorrow night I'm doing nothing because I have nothing going on, and Sunday church stuff." My brilliant reply was, "Oh, that sounds nice. Have a good weekend." He turned, and as I watched him walked away I realized he was hinting about hanging out, and I had totally missed it. I was kicking myself.

I prayed again, "Oh Lord, please have him try again and ask me out." Two minutes later he came back to my desk and asked, "So what else are you doing besides . . ." and repeated my first list of things I said I was going to do. Incredibly brainless me said, "Oh I think I'll go shopping, too." He responded, "Oh." He turned and walked away. As I realized I had screwed up such an obvious hint to go out I was screaming at myself inside my head. I was so mad I had screwed up again. But then I realized I had prayed that he would ask me out. He didn't. He just hinted around. I decided to accept that God's answer was no and let it go.

On that Saturday night, which I spent alone at home, I wrote a song that I ended up performing in coffeehouses, and a good number of people told me it was their favorite song of mine. One time I performed it at a singles group, and a divorced woman whose last child had just moved out cried through the whole performance. She was feeling lonely, and my song comforted her. After I wrote the song I could see that I was doing just what I was supposed to do that night, creating something special.

After my infatuation with the guy died, I saw that he really was not a good fit for me, and I was very thankful I never dated him. He and I ended up marrying different people, and we both were very happy with our choices and stayed friends for years. Not dating my coworker turned out to be the best move after all. So maybe I wasn't as dumb as I thought. Here are the lyrics of the song I wrote that night:

Never-Ending Friend

1. When I am discouraged, when I'm all alone,
   When I fear the future and all the unknown
   I think of a friend, a never-ending friend.
   His name is Jesus, my never-ending friend.
   He never goes away from me.
   His love will never end.
   I love my Jesus. I love him, yeah, I do.
   And if you open up your heart
   He'll be a never-ending friend to you.

2. He's always looking over me. He's always there.
   He's always thinking of me.
   He feels my every care.
   Oh, how He loves me.
   His name is Jesus. My never-ending friend.
   He's always looking over me.
   His love will never end.
   So many times I forget him. He never forgets me.
   I'm thankful for his constant love
   and faithful security.

3. Though one day I may lose my mind
   or all of my health.
   Or one day I may lose my job or all of my wealth,
   There is one thing, I will never lose.
   His name is Jesus, my never-ending friend.
   He never goes away from me.
   His love will never end.
   On him I rest my confidence, on Him I lay my life.
   I will live with Him in peace and through strife.

No Story for You

      Although I had a lot of crushes on various men I worked with over my career, and I'm sure from time to time people gossiped about me and who they thought I was "doing," the real story is I never had sex with anyone who worked at any of the companies at which I worked. I know, what a boring geek. It just seemed to me to be a bad idea to date people with whom I had to work. Most romantic relationships don't result in lifelong matrimony. In other words, most of them end. I didn't want to work with someone who I used to date, and to have that awkward uncomfortableness looming as I tried to talk about work with a serious face. All my romances have been with nice men I met outside of work, and when we said our good byes, I didn't have to look at their faces anymore. It worked for me, although it doesn't make for exciting book material. Hence, we move along to the next topic.

Chapter 10

Memorable Business Trips

Enjoying the Pool in Houston

A group of us had to travel to our Houston office to install software we had written, put it into production, and run conversion programs to convert all the data to the new system. The conversion jobs would run for hours in the old days. We would kick them off at night, then go have dinner, go to bed, sleep in, sit around the pool, and then go in the afternoon to check on our jobs. It was a tough life. But one day we went in and found that all our load programs had abruptly aborted. Turns out the cleaning person thought the big red emergency fire button in the

data center was a light switch and cut off all the power to the computer room. We were so happy: another day of pool sitting for us! Ah, now that was a good business trip.

Cheating on the Expense Report

My coworkers taught young me how to inflate an expense report to make extra cash on a work trip. You write down that you took a limo to the airport but have a friend or your spouse take you, you write down an expense for breakfast, but then buy milk and cereal and eat in the room, and so on. I was just out of college and kind of a wuss, so I went along with my cheating older coworkers. But I also read my Bible every day, and darn it, every day I kept seeing verses like "ill gain profits none." I mean I was really getting it from God. So finally on the third trip like this I decided to not lie and turned in a truthful expense report. The boss called the other three into his office and chewed them out. Without meaning to, I had gotten my coworkers in trouble. But I knew I did what I needed to do. And I never inflated my expense report again. God taught me a good lesson. It feels good to be honest.

An Adventure to Austin

I was asked to present in our Austin office at 1:00 p.m. My flight was in the morning of the same day. The limo driver didn't show. When I called the limo company, I learned that they had gotten my address wrong, and the driver was lost. He finally arrived and took me to the airport, but I missed my flight. I jumped on the next plane to Austin. In Texas, I had the taxi take me straight to the office. I arrived fifteen minutes before my meeting time, downed a quick salad, and gave my presentation. I was proud of myself that I had figured out a way to make it there on time even with this severe left turn. After that trip, however, I made it a policy to always fly the day before I needed to meet with people. Stuff happens, and it's best to have extra time for stuff.

Not Quite There

I was working on a project where we were converting customer data for our Australian stores into our global database. We needed to travel to Sydney to meet with our business partners in order to work out all the details of the project. Four of us from our US office were approved to travel. I decided to extend my stay and visit some of the beauty of the country, plus bring my husband and niece along with me.

We arrived at our local city airport and learned at the counter that Australia had a visa requirement. None of our travel agencies had informed us of this requirement, including my corporate travel agency. Australia provides a website on which we attempted to get this necessary clearance via our smart phones while at the airport. We were able to do so for three of the six of us. But the other three of us, including me, couldn't get the system to accept us. One of us had help from the airline staff at the counter, and they got her approval. But I was going on a different airline, and their airport staff told me I was on my own. After two hours of entering and reentering my information into the website, I still had not received an approval email.

The airport staff then finally helped me. They told me their system showed that I finally had approval, but now it was too late to catch the flight, and they had no more flights that night. Another airline had a flight, but it was taking off in an hour, and we were not even in that airline's terminal, plus we'd have to get our luggage checked, go through security, and so on. And we'd have to buy new tickets for that flight, and they were outrageously priced. We were out of luck and had to go home. My boss and another coworker did the same. Only one of our group of six got to travel to Sydney.

On the two days of meetings, I had to work from 6:00 p.m. to 1:00 a.m. in order to meet with the Australian partners over the Internet. We made it work, but I never saw their faces, let alone meet them and build relationships with them. The whole experience was deeply disappointing to me, especially because I had lost out on a good amount of personal funds and a lot of time planning a vacation for my family. I spent many hours in the days and weeks that followed working to get partial refunds and credits, which I was able to obtain, and which relieved some of the disappointment. I took off those days I was planning on traveling as a nice stay-cation with my husband, and that is also when I wrote most of this book, so all was not lost. My boss complained to the department that chose the travel agency, but the complaints fell on deaf ears, and the company made no real changes.

In general, companies have decided that computers suffice and that humans are no longer needed. We had to book everything through computer websites, without humans to make sure everything was in order. Their sites didn't send the visa notifications to us as they should have. We had to get visas via a website that was poorly written and provided no access to humans who could help us through the process. This reliance on systems victimized the customer instead of providing value. Business was harmed, our vacation was lost, and companies made money and provided nothing for that money.

I filed complaints against the three travel agencies I had used with the Better Business Bureau and spent hours on the phone with the airlines. Humans then provided the refunds and credits. Humans, not computers, made it better.

Fast Shopper

We had flown to Toronto for a meeting with another company to learn about a system they were using and to evaluate whether we would want to use it as well. We decided it was not a good fit. We had about an hour at the high-rise office building before we needed to leave for the airport. I took advantage of the time and hit the stores in the building. I purchased a beautiful maroon suit with a silk blouse for three hundred dollars. When I met up with my coworker, he couldn't believe I was able to buy a nice suit in that one hour of time. Never underestimate the power of a career woman in a mall.

Deceiving Business Trip

My company sent about twenty of us to Orlando to attend a huge technical conference. The conference was sponsored by a vendor of a product we used, and like many technology vendors who sponsor such conferences, they provided a lot of good food, drink, and fun for the participants. The last night of the conference the entire Islands of Adventure theme park was open only to those of us attending the conference, so we had the place to ourselves. We giggled like teenagers as we rode the rides together without waiting in any lines.

Only a few weeks after this big, fancy trip, I was surprised to find out that two people who were in our posse were laid off in the next wave of cuts. I remembered their smiling faces as they walked around the park, and I pondered how they may have been deceived into thinking the company considered them valuable enough to invest in them with that week of education—only to find out that they were on the next list of cuts.

It was a sobering lesson to me and taught me to never feel too sure about anything. In one minute a company can send a person on a fun and educational trip, and in the next minute it can lay off the same person. It's best to keep myself marketable, keep the resume up-to-date, and be ready for anything. And I have been.

Travel, travel, travel

The technology field has allowed me to travel to many wonderful cities, mostly to attend or present at computer conferences. Cities of conferences where I have presented over my career include Chicago, Boston, Denver, Austin, Salt Lake City, Des Moines, London, Copenhagen, Oslo, and Sao Paolo. I've also attended conferences in Washington, DC, Las Vegas, Orlando, New Orleans, Kansas City, San Jose, and San Diego, and I have worked in Houston, Austin, Toronto, Amsterdam, Munich, and London (but not Sydney!). The technology field definitely has its perks, and travel is one of them. It pays to be a geek.

Speaking at a conference in Sao Paolo

Speaking in Oslo

Dinner after meetings in Amsterdam

Me skiing after presenting at a conference in Salt Lake City

Chapter 11

Especially Memorable Layoffs and Relocations

No-Access Layoff

My company was having layoffs. A very nice friend of mine had been an administrative assistant for the company for many years—I think about twenty or so. She came in and tried to log into her desktop computer, and she couldn't get into the system. She went to her boss and told him. He said "sit down," and he let her know she was being let go. The poor woman found out by losing her access. She walked out, and none of us saw or heard from her ever again. I always felt so bad for her. How hard that must have been. I missed her too. She was the nicest lady. The business world can be very cold. Since then, when layoffs are looming, I have a personal little celebration when I'm able to log into my computer in the morning.

Third Strike and He Was Out

In another layoff at another company where I worked there was a guy in finance who had health problems, and his wife had just left him. Then he was laid off. He killed himself. That was the only time I know of when someone committed suicide after a layoff. But ever since, with every layoff I have worried because I know how devastating they can be to people. I always tell people positive things too. There is always a better way.

Good Advice

My workload was quite heavy, and I felt I needed a second person who knew how to do my job so I could share some of my workload. I asked my boss for help. Rather than hiring someone who had experience in my field, she opted to have me train another woman on our team. I agreed. However, after the trainee started attempting to do my work, I could see that she wasn't interested in learning from me. I found out that without consulting with me, she had modified the design I had been working on in a radical way. It was as if I had designed a beautiful mountain chalet with natural wood shake siding, and she added onto it a garage with bright pink vinyl siding. It worked, but it violated other values that allowed for better design choices.

I went to my boss and asked her to encourage the new trainee to collaborate with me. My boss said she would talk to her, but the boss failed to follow through. I complained again, and the boss threatened me by telling me I needed to just deal with it or it would be reflected on my annual review. I went to her boss to complain, and he listened empathetically but said he would rather my manager deal with the issue and did nothing to resolve the conflict. So I pulled off a great acting job by pretending that I had let it go when I was steaming mad inside, and I spent my energies looking for a new job. The day after I gave my boss my notice she called in sick. I guess I had surprised her. Her failure to resolve the issues meant she lost the only senior-level person in my field on her team.

I had worked for that company for thirteen years. An older coworker who had had more job changes than me gave me some great advice I have shared with others many times over my career. He said, "Starting new job is like a three- to six-month PMS. Some days you feel good about the new job, some days you think you made a big mistake, some days you feel nervous, some confident. You just have to ride out that initial period, and in time you will feel OK about the job." His advice helped me calm myself as I adjusted to all the changes the new company brought.

One year after I left the former company, they laid off nearly every person in the entire office, reducing staff from about one thousand people in Chicago to only five, and moving all the surviving jobs to the Houston location. They didn't even provide job transfers to the staff. When I learned about this, I understood why my boss hadn't supported my long-term values: she may have sensed that the whole place was at risk. I was very glad I moved on before the chaos hit. I was also able to hire some of the laid-off folks at my new company, as I was a hiring manager with open positions. I made some great friends at the first company whom I still hang out with now, decades later. And I kept that company's stock, which I had received in my 401K, and it has grown more in value than any other investment in my portfolio. That company caused me temporary personal stress, but in the long run it provided great friends and a comfortable retirement. I'm glad I worked there, and I look back on it now with the peaceful perspective of knowing how it all worked together for my good in the long run.

The Layoff Battleground

My department layoff day hit. This one was in May 1993. At 9:00 a.m. all the doors of the managers' offices closed—one, two, three, four. A few minutes later people walked out and were escorted to the conference room in the corner, and then escorted out of the building. Someone came up and asked the guy to my left to go to the boss's office. Then the guy on my right. I felt like layoff bombs were going off all around me. We were all shell-shocked and couldn't do anything but watch and feel scared and sad. Synchronized firings are shit to watch.

Companies Move

Four out of the five companies I have worked for have relocated their headquarters at least once. The first company moved from Chicago to Lombard, Illinois, when I worked there in 1986, and then after I left, it relocated its headquarters to Houston, and then back again to Lombard. The third company I worked for had moved from Chicago to Hoffman Estates, Illinois, before I joined the company, and while I was there the company was purchased, and the buying company's employees were forced to resign or move from Detroit to Hoffman Estates. The fourth company I worked at had already located from Toronto to Naperville, Illinois, before I joined, and after I left they moved from Naperville to Cincinnati. The fifth company moved from Chicago to Oak Brook, Illinois, in the early 1970s before I started, and while I was there it moved back from Oak Brook to Chicago. I can't say that for any of these moves I saw an improvement in stock price or cost savings, although they could have been there and I was just not privy to these benefits. In all of the changes I saw people leave and find new jobs. I learned that nothing is necessarily permanent—not a job, not a company location, and not even a company. I realized that I have to change with the changes to be successful.

Glad I Said "No Thanks"

I was a team leader of four fellow data architects. The company was reorganizing our department for about the tenth time in five years. I was asked if I wanted to be promoted to be the manager of a team of twelve data architects. I knew if I took that role I could no longer do any design work, which I enjoyed and preferred. I also thought not using my technical skills would cause me to be less marketable. I turned down the opportunity. The next layoff, the man who took that manager position was laid off, along with his boss, his boss's boss, and his boss's boss's boss, all the way to the vice president level. It paid off well for me to not take that promotion. IT management is a much riskier career path than being a technical expert.

My Boss Du Jour

At one company I had twelve bosses in six years. They loved to reorganize, and it was as though they could never make up their minds or get it right. We had a joke that if you didn't like your boss, you didn't need to worry, you'd get a new one soon.

The Birthday List

In one layoff I experienced, a layoff spreadsheet was leaked out of HR and spread like wildfire throughout the company. It was the list of people about to lose their jobs. There were no names on the list, but job titles and birth dates. Everyone checked the list to see if their birthdate and position was listed, and if it was, they hoped there was another person exactly their same age doing a similar job to them, or they just updated their resume and prepared for the axe. I suppose the person who leaked the list should have gotten the axe, but we were all glad to know our fate before it hit. If you ask me, that person should have been promoted.

What Happens after a Buyout

Three of the five companies I worked for were bought by another company. For the first two, I saw that there was the same pattern after the buyout: rounds of layoffs—more than seven—and then an office closing. When I was at the third company that was bought, my husband was in treatment for cancer and was not able to work much. My income and health benefits were essential to his survival. I wasn't going to take my chances. The day the company informed us employees of the buyout I put my resume on the job boards and started looking for a new job. That was a Friday, and by the following Monday I was talking to companies. I was able to find an ideal new position within about two months and left. My former coworkers were still in denial and thought I had overreacted. One year later everyone in that office was laid off, and they closed the location. A coworker even called me for a lead on a position. I recommended him, but he didn't get the job. Sometimes companies make changes that are good for the stockholders and higher-ups, and whether we like it or not, we employees just have to move on. And so I have. The nice thing about being a technical professional is I've always been able to find a good job quickly when I've needed to.

My Roller Coaster Ride

I have been through well over twenty layoffs in my career and have never been laid off myself, although I've been nervous many times. But I have been promoted eight times to a first-line manager of some sort: team leader, manager, senior project manager—a lot of different titles. And after being promoted to these positions in some reorganizations, in subsequent ones I was demoted eight times to being an individual contributor with no direct reports. Yes, eight times promoted and then demoted. Companies go from times when they want to create career paths for their employees, to times when they want a flatter organizational structure. My position changed with each new leader's philosophy. After the seventh time I promised myself I would not accept a first-line manager position ever again. And then I had to. And then they did it to me again.

Most of these were done in a mass change—all of us first-liners were demoted together. And they usually tried to sell it not as a demotion but just less work for equal pay. But at other times some boss was just moving around people in his or her own little world.

If I had really wanted to be in management, I could have been. But I know myself. I like to make things. Create things. I am happier doing hands-on work rather than submitting budget numbers, reporting the status of other people's work, pushing people to get their jobs done, and so on. I also know that technical skills are more sought-after than management experience, and I have always wanted to keep my hands-on knowledge sharp and marketable.

At this point in my career I am just enjoying being where I am and embracing it. Not everyone is happiest being a boss. And I have learned that I can lead people by helping them with what I know rather than by telling them what to do. In a way, I have more influence now because it results from my knowledge, not my position. Climbing the management track is not the only way for a person to advance in their career, especially in the IT field, where technical leadership is valued more than people leadership.

Chapter 12

Memorable Work Golf Outings

Tragic Lesson for Us Golfers

A group of guys from work went out golfing together. One guy brought his son. He let his son walk ahead of him before he teed off, and the drive went right into the boy's head. The child was rushed to the hospital with a serious injury. He recovered, but the dad struggled for a long time to forgive himself.

When I learned of this I made sure I never advanced ahead of someone in golf, no matter how good they were. Everyone has a stray shot occasionally, and rushing ahead is just not worth it. Don't take that chance, my golfing friends.

Surprise Win

I was golfing with some of the guys at our annual technology golf outing. We were at a short hole, about a hundred yards. I hit a nice one with my five wood. The men jumped up and down and yelled in celebration over my shot. I said, "What, what? What are you so excited about?" They told me, "You got closest to pin! You got closest to pin!" I said, "What is closest to pin?" I wasn't an experienced golfer at that point. They explained that this was a prize hole, and the person who got the ball closest to the pin in one shot would win something. I ended up being the closest of the day and won a putter engraved with the company logo. It wasn't a great putter but it was so fun that I actually beat all the guys that day. Honestly, it was a total fluke. I've never been considered a coordinated person. But I guess I was that day.

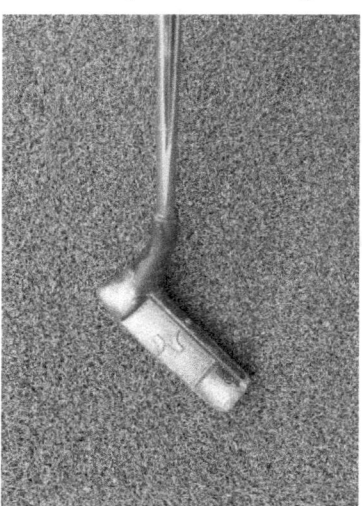

Putter I won

A Sexy Promise

My husband and I were golfing with two other guys at a work-sponsored annual golf outing. My husband wasn't a great golfer but was trying his best. Most of his hits were not very good. Near the end of our eighteen holes I whispered into his ear, "If you hit this good honey," and I promised him special sexual favors if could hit the ball well. His next hit was a long, straight, perfectly executed shot—his best of the day. We cracked up knowing what had motivated my husband. The other guys asked, "What did you say to him?" My husband and I just looked at each other, smiled big, said nothing, and laughed.

Chapter 13

The Old Days

Don't Forget the Rubber Band

In college all of our computer programs were entered into the mainframe via punch cards. And most of our assignments had to be timestamped by midnight to get credit. Being a last-minute person at that time in my life, I did a lot of programming and punch card typing in the night. Fifteen minutes before midnight I was about ready to submit my final program to the mainframe via the card reader. Then the kid in front of me put a deck in the reader with a rubber band still around his cards. The lone input machine was jammed and none of us could submit our programs. Geeks were swearing at the poor kid. I made a note to myself, "Always be sure you remove your rubber band if you want to survive the computer science program."

Me holding punch cards

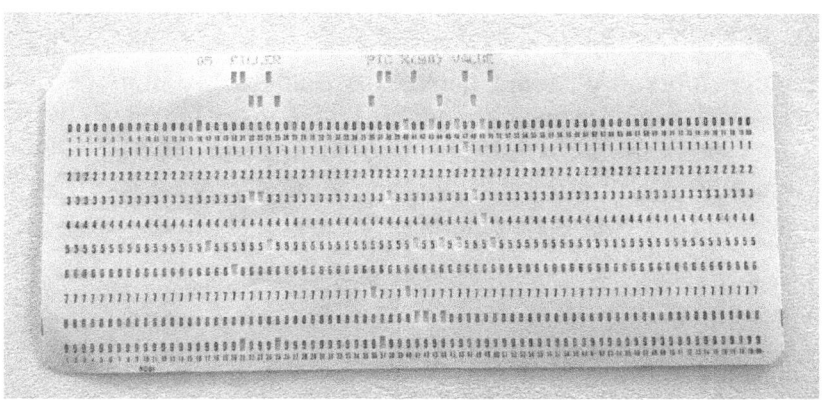
Single Punch Card

Burgers before Computers

In 1976, when I turned sixteen, I started working as a crew member at my local McDonald's restaurant. There wasn't a computer in the entire place. We took orders with a pad of paper and a pen and had all the product prices memorized. We calculated the five percent sales tax in our heads. We all knew how to make change and did so very quickly. Inventory and financials were all tracked on this stuff called paper.

Today so much is automated and computerized, people find it hard to believe that not long ago we used to do business without computers. But we did. We managed to cook food, serve it, charge people, and track it all without these devices. I'm sure the number of customers per hour were much lower than today, however, and the number of items on the menu has increased because customers want much more. Consumer demand caused us to automate to provide variety, speed, and cost savings. But if all the computers of the world were to go down, the old folks like me who used to do it all without computers would still be able to feed you. If that happens, come by my house and I'll keep you alive.

Me working at McDonald's as a teen

The Way a Computer Geek Parties All Night Long

Some kids in school would party all night. Not geeky nerdy me. I would come into my dorm room at 6:00 a.m. after working literally all night in the computer lab getting my code perfect. My art major roommate would look at me like I was from outer space. But hey, I had a good GPA and landed a job before I graduated, so I am glad I made that choice.

Me in college in the dorm

Me and my college roommate

The Real Old Days

When I first started my programming career in 1982, I worked with a man who was about sixty years old. He talked about his early days when writing a computer program involved moving wires around on a circuitry board. It was so early in the computer age, no programming languages existed. This predated punch cards too. It is still hard for me to imagine how difficult it must have been to write equations and produce a report by hard-wiring a computer's logic. But he did it early in his career. Although I started programming when the field was still relatively young, there were a lot of smart pioneers like him who found a way to automate logic with very limited computers. All of us IT geeks are still pioneers in an ever-changing new profession. That's part of the fun.

Older coworker who hard-wired code

Rewriting Code Over and Over

When I started my programming career we were on the mainframe. Three years later a new microprocessor by the Wang company came out, and we had to rewrite all our code on the Wang. Turns out the Wang didn't work so well. Three years later we were writing the code again on the mainframe, this time using IDMS. That didn't last long, and three years later we wrote it again using Sybase and PowerBuilder. And I'm sure that code has been written over and over again since.

We still have to do this today, except that sometimes the code lasts a little longer—more like five to seven years. But still, this is what we do in IT a lot: just keep rewriting the same programs with the same logic but with newer, better technology. It's a relatively young field and rapidly changing, so we have all learned to go with the flow. And it's likely we are about to rewrite code again next year with the system I now work on. In a rapidly changing field, some things never change.

The Business Casual Friday Committee

I worked at a bank that was so conservative they had six months of meetings to decide if we could have business casual Fridays. Finally, they approved, so the ladies could wear slacks on Fridays, and the men got to take off their ties. I had worked previously at a company where we could wear jeans five days a week if we liked, so I found the bank's extreme fear of casual dress quite surprising. But that's the banking industry. I never felt I fit in with that culture, and I didn't last long there. I need my jeans.

Smoking in the Old Days

It used to be acceptable to smoke not only inside the office building, but also at our desks and in meetings. Around 1993 my company decided to change some conference rooms to nonsmoking meeting rooms. The smokers were mad they couldn't just smoke anywhere they liked. One guy started smoking in protest. We had signs on the doors to the conference rooms, indicating whether they were smoking or nonsmoking meeting spaces. How things have changed! And since I have always been a nonsmoker, how glad I am.

An Early Lesson in Estimation

I was at about year three of my career, and my boss asked me to meet with an entire engineering department, find out everything they wanted us to do for them, and estimate the work required to meet each request. I dove in and did the interviews and estimates, then sent them to the team and my boss. The department decided that all but one of the requests would require too much work to be worth the time, and they asked us to work on just one of the projects on the list. I felt bad about it and doubted myself, so I asked my boss, "Were my estimates too high?" He told me, "No, not at all. You did exactly what I wanted you to do. They need to know how much work it is, and if it's not worth the time, we shouldn't do that work. This is a good thing." It was a great lesson for me in telling the truth in estimates, and I learned that not doing some projects can be the best decision.

I wish I could say this was common practice in my field, but it has rarely been done. Usually management tells us to do a huge amount of work in a small amount of time without first comparing the costs to the expected benefits to see if it's worth the time. And then when the due dates are not hit, they get upset like we are all lazy, time-wasting workers. If they would let us tell them the truth in the beginning, weighing the value of the project against the time investment, we would be doing the best work possible. But I guess that is too logical for people who oversee people who write computer logic.

In the Beginning

When I was in high school, I told my dad I wanted to be a math teacher, since math was my best subject. Dad was a high school vocational and industrial arts teacher. He said, "Don't be a teacher! It's a dead-end job." "What should I do then?," I asked. Dad's experience meant he had a deep understanding of the teenage mind. He knew we kids don't like to listen to our parents. So instead of just telling me what he likely already knew, he said, "Go to your math teacher and ask him what jobs are out there right now for a person who is good at math." I did just that. My math teacher told me there were lots of jobs in engineering and computer science that people who are good at math would likely do well in. After high school, when I went to our local junior college, I took classes in both areas. I didn't like advanced physics, but I loved programming. I knew that was the path for me. And I have been very happy with my career. I guess Father does know best.

Typing Class

My grandmother advised me to take a typing class in high school because she wanted me to have what she believed to be a marketable skill. She said, "Don't plan to be dependent on a man. I've seen women who were, and their husband passed away and they had a hard time providing for themselves." I told Grandma I planned to go to college and get a good job. But I still decided to follow her advice and I took a typing class in summer school.

My typing teacher had only one hand, and yet taught us two handed typing. He did it very well too. Being able to type has turned out to be quite the asset for me as a programmer. I have typed every day of my career. And providing for myself has also been extremely valuable, especially because my first husband passed away from cancer. Grandma had a prophetic word of advice for me, and I'm so grateful I followed her words of wisdom. God was looking out for me that day.

Learning a Lesson

When I was a young data architect, I designed databases in a puristic style called third normal form. I was trained do to this, and it was all I knew how to do at first. Later I learned what we call denormalization, where we make changes to the puristic design so people find it easier to write programs and so that retrieving data from the database would work faster.

The programmer working with the puristic database I had designed came to me one day and asked me if I knew how to code for a requirement she had from her business partner, who was using my design. I was not able to write the code, and neither could she. The puristic style made the code extremely complex. She taught me such a great lesson that day. I never left a design in the puristic state after that, but always tuned and tweaked for performance and ease of use.

Two companies later I had created a great design, using the experience I had acquired over the years. A younger guy who thought he was smarter than me complained that I had strayed from purism and therefore was wrong. I went on vacation, and when I returned I found out that he had modified my design, making it puristic, and had convinced the project manager to implement his design. I was not happy to find out he had used my absence to force his way upon my work, and I knew he made it worse, not better. But his ego would not allow him to learn from me.

After the design was implemented, one of my business partners asked me to pull information from the design. I knew the code would be very difficult because it was too puristic. I asked the guy who had modified my design to pull the information, and he was unable to. He looked embarrassed, and I hope he realized why I had designed it as I had.

Stinky Program

When I first started working in the engineering computer division of a natural gas company, I was told my coworkers had just finished a project to convert all of our programs so they could be stored on the mainframe instead of on punched cards. My coworker pointed to one big deck of cards and said, "We decided to not bother converting this program. This is a program that computes how to create natural methane gas out of cow manure. Turns out it really isn't something we wanted to pursue once we studied it because it wasn't profitable." They called it the Poo Program.

Chapter 14

More Interesting Stories

Claims Computer Geeks Can Falsely Make

My husband and I suspected that his son was using my work computer to view online porn. One night we came home early from our normal date night. Instead of going into the house, my husband snuck around the back and spied in the office window. Sure enough, his young teen boy was looking at porn on my computer. We waited until several days later, and my husband told his son that we had figured out he was watching porn on my computer, claiming that I had some fancy spyware that enabled me to know—a total lie. But the kid didn't know the difference. My husband told him that he understood that it's natural to find that tempting, but we did not want him looking at porn using my work computer. The kid was good and stopped using that computer for that purpose. But I wouldn't doubt that he found another way. He was resourceful. And using a lie, so were we.

Messy Meter

One year, between Christmas and New Year's while most people were on vacation, I came in and I spent the whole week cleaning my very messy, cluttered office. When my boss returned after the holiday break, he told me, "It won't last." He knew my love for paper and piles. I decided he was right, and I needed some help to keep my office clean. So, I created a "Messy Meter," which I posted on the outside of my office, so others could let me know when little Miss Piggy needed to do a cleaning. My coworkers got into it and often turned the meter to the red zone when it started getting bad again. Wish I could say it cured me of my clutter habit, but it didn't. But it did give us a little fun at work—mostly my coworkers making fun of me, that is.

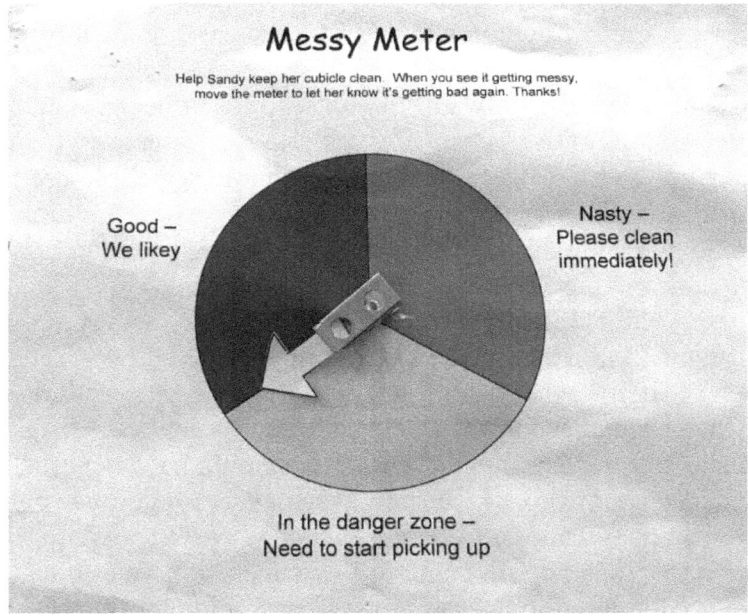

Messy Meter

Triplet Ice Cream

At my first job after college, occasionally the team I worked with organized a little walk in the midafternoon in the summer. We'd stroll together down Michigan Avenue in Chicago, where the office was located, to a little ice cream shop owned and run by three identical triplet Asian women. These ladies were energetic and eager to please us with their yummy frozen treats. Seeing the three matching ladies was more of a draw for us than the actual ice cream, although their product was quite good. Taking a break to go get ice cream is always a good idea, especially if triplets are involved.

What a Waste

Another common and frustrating experience most of us in IT share is working hard to write and deliver a new computer system only to have the whole project canceled after months or even years of work. This has happened to me four times that I can remember. Technology people are in high demand and are paid a good salary. You would think a company would be very careful not to waste such scarce and expensive talent. But over and over, companies do.

After this happened the first time I was very upset because I knew people had worked overtime and weekends to try to deliver the system, and then all our work was thrown away when the company reorganized. A new person had taken over the department our system would have benefited, and this person thought the new system was not going to help the company enough to be worth using. We wondered how the new person could come to this conclusion. We thought we had already shown how the system would yield a positive return for the company. Didn't matter though.

Most of the subsequent times this happened, it was for similar reasons: a new person took over and deemed the system we were building not worth continuing. We worked hard and took pride in our work, so none of these project cancellations were easy to accept. But we must accept them to be in this field. So we do.

How Learning Has Changed

After my husband passed away following a long battle with cancer, I found I had a lot of time on my hands. Because I am a true geek at heart, I decided it would be fun to learn to write iPhone apps. I took a couple of courses at my local junior college to update my technical skills in this area.

There I was, an older student coding side by side with teenage boys. I noticed the kids didn't write down a word the teacher said, while I typed notes into my laptop like a stenographer. "How are these kids going to learn this?" I wondered. I was surprised that their learning style was to get the PowerPoint slides from the teacher and then do what slides said to do. They didn't pay much attention to the teacher's verbal explanations.

On the days we had to turn in our programs, I watched some of these boys scrambling to get their code done, and not looking calm. A good number of the younger people didn't seem to do well in the class, and we older folks were all getting straight As. From my observation, if these kids had learned to listen and apply the teacher's explanations, they might have done better. When did teaching and learning evolve into this very passive, disconnected method? Is this a result of their world of disconnection because the younger generation mostly talks through computer devices? Perhaps.

I am thinking of going back into teaching computer courses after I retire from my full-time technology career. But I'm not sure I will know how to help these kids learn. Why even give a lecture if they basically ignore you? It'd almost be better to just hand them instructions and assignments and make every class a time I am available if they get stuck. Good God, if teachers had done that to me when I was in school I would never have graduated. The new generation is going to bring on a new world, that's for sure. This baby boomer is going to need some patience and maybe a lot of wine.

Big Business Benefits

I worked for a large corporation that was a major sponsor of the Chicago Cubs. I have to think that arrangement is why the company choir I was part of was accepted to sing the National Anthem at a Cubs game. We really weren't that good. But there we were, walking on the holy ground of Chicago baseball, Wrigley Field, on national TV, singing that patriotic anthem. We were thrilled to have the opportunity. Just another cool adventure I had thanks to my career in a major company.

In another very large company where I worked we had a gospel choir. The company was a sponsor of the show *Singsation*. I'm sure that helped us get a gig on the show. That choir wasn't great either, but there we were, behind a huge boom mic and cameras, on that great Chicago gospel show.

My career in IT has been quite the adventure, and these two choirs and TV events were two of the highlights for sure. I never thought when I was learning to code in college that I would end up having such special opportunities. But working in the technology field has given me a lot of significant moments. Geeks do have fun.

Singing at Wrigley

Me at Wrigley

Choir on Singsation

Watching the End

Two of the companies I have worked at were purchased by another company while I was there. In both events, I snuck into the shareholders meeting where they ended the original company's official existence, including when the longstanding Sears, Roebuck and Company ceased to exist under that long-standing household name, as it was purchased by the newly formed Sears Holdings Company. The rich large-percentage stockholders who dared to attend these meetings were very well-dressed and wore wide smiles. The retirees lined up at the microphone to protest. The meeting facilitator worked to cut off the discussion and quickly get the purchase agreement concluded. As I sat in these meetings I felt sad to see a company end that I knew many had worked hard to build. But I also felt special that I could witness history. Even sad history.

Sobering Information

In 1986 I was in my grad school class Computers and Society, one of my favorite classes. The professor explained how our personal information was being shared among all the major institutions, such as employers, marketers, various branches of the government, and more. He talked about how this sharing and marrying of our information is powerful to those who have it, and how they can use it for good or to harm us. He also told us how a satellite could clearly read a credit card, and that there had been experimentation with putting computer chips in people and being able to scan them. All this is power that could be used for good, or in the wrong hands, for harm. I was so stirred hearing all of this that in class I wrote a long poem, "Little Chip" (below), and read it to the class at the end. The class was surprised that I had created an entire long poem in that session.

As I have watched the birth of grocery store scanners, powerful phone apps, GPS trackers on everything, and cameras everywhere, I remember my teacher's lesson of how this can all be good, but if in the wrong hands, very bad. The Bible says that in the future, people of faith will be persecuted, and they will not be able to buy and sell without "the mark of the beast." Could the little chip under the skin be the avenue of the mark? Will this be used someday to persecute people who believe in a way others believe to be not tolerable? I hate to say it, but I can see that happening someday. I just hope I'm long gone when it does, and our children do the right thing. God help them. Computers can be powerful weapons if used in such a way. We have a responsibility to use them for good. I choose the path of good.

Little Chip

(March 3, 1986)

There is a little chip.
It has your name.
You must have it
to play the game.

It has your number
and your shoe size.
It has your credit level
and the color of your eyes.

It knows your diseases.
It knows your wife.
It knows your children.
It knows your whole life.

It's embedded in your fingers.
It's written on your head.
And because you have it
your children are fed.

But there's one problem
with this nifty little device.
Although it looks so very helpful
in reality, it's not so nice.

For it's not just the chip that knows
what you've been up to these days.
No, it's the one with power who knows
and he's the one who says

Whether it's OK or not.
And if he doesn't like what you do

You'll find yourself hungry and cold
and eventually you're through.

What if the one with power
doesn't like the way you dress?
What if he says your religion
is a problem and a pest?

What if he says he's God
or that he's Jesus Christ?
Are you going to surrender
to this poltergeist?

According to the Bible
this is meant to be.
There will be no way out,
nowhere to flee.

And those who receive "the mark,"
 the tiny little chip,
Will find themselves
in evil's grip.

They will be asked to deny their faith
so we all can get along.
And if they don't
they can't possibly belong.

What will you do
on this approaching day?
What will you say?
Decide now
because it isn't far away.

Will you change your religion?

Will you deny the Lord?
Are you willing to pay the price?
Is it something you can afford?

Jesus said if you want to live
you must lose your life.
You must be willing to deny yourself
through peace and through strife.

I can only hope and pray
that I'll be faithful to the end
Even if it means suffering,
even if I haven't a human friend.

For this life is passing away.
There's a better home, I know,
And it's worth any price I must pay.
His way, I plan to go.

Whether it means a nice life on Earth
or suffering and death
I will not deny my Lord
though it takes my very last breath.

www.ingramcontent.com/pod-product-compliance
Lightning Source LLC
Chambersburg PA
CBHW070303010526
44108CB00039B/1701